READING THE RAV

EXPLORING RELIGIOUS
THEMES IN THE THOUGHT OF
RABBI JOSEPH B. SOLOVEITCHIK

DR. MOSHE SOKOLOW

KODESH PRESS

Reading the Rav:
Exploring Religious Themes in the Thought of
Rabbi Joseph B. Soloveitchik

© Moshe Sokolow 2018
ISBN: 978-1-947857-05-6
Paperback edition

About the Cover

Cover image courtesy of Joel Schreiber, Chairman of the Board of Rabbi Isaac Elchanan Theological Seminary. Photograph is of Rabbi Soloveitchik leading *sheva berakhot* at Chairman Schreiber's wedding in 1961. This photograph is one of the few items rescued from a fire that consumed most of Mr. Schreiber's apartment.

The Publisher extends its gratitude to
Mr. Laurence Goldstein for his help editing this work.

Published & Distributed by
Kodesh Press L.L.C.
New York, NY
www.KodeshPress.com
sales@kodeshpress.com

TABLE OF CONTENTS

THE RAV

A PERSONAL INTRODUCTION

The title "The Rav," literally: the Master, attests to the status of Rabbi Joseph B. Soloveitchik (1903-1993) as the preeminent teacher of those Jews in both the United States and around the world who are known as modern Orthodox. His mastery of both traditional talmudic-halakhic scholarship and modern philosophy, a pedagogy that engaged students intellectually and spiritually, and a felicitous style of both oral and literary presentation made the Rav a byword in Orthodox Jewish law and lore for more than half a century.

Upon his arrival in the United States from Berlin in 1932, Soloveitchik assumed the title of chief rabbi of Boston, where he also founded the Maimonides Day School, whose K-12 coeducational curriculum (girls and boys study even Talmud together) he personally oversaw. In his more than 40-year tenure as *rosh yeshivah* (rabbinical dean) of Yeshiva University's Rabbi Isaac Elchanan Theological Seminary in New York, it ordained more rabbis than any other comparable institution in modern times. Soloveitchik's intellectual attainments include 40 years of daily *shi'urim* (classes) and frequent public lectures, whose audiences, drawn by his consummate homiletic skills, included rabbinical students, ordained rabbis, educators, social workers, mental health workers, and just plain *balabatim* (lay people). A typical *derashah* (lecture) would combine the elucidation of a complex halakhic problem with the clarification of an abstract philosophical concept delivered in fluent, idiomatic English, or an even more fluent Yiddish that bordered, frequently, on the lyrical.

A hereditary perfectionist—scion of a rabbinical dynasty notorious for its literary reticence—Rabbi Soloveitchik published relatively little in his lifetime. His halakhic contributions are largely posthumous collections edited by his students. His philosophical discourses, however, appeared in his lifetime either as books or as monographs in *Tradition* magazine. His many public lectures have been published in Hebrew translation, and, most recently, Meotzar Horav, a foundation headed by former students, has overseen the publication of a dozen thematic anthologies based on his published and unpublished writings.

In the fall of 1985, I returned to Yeshiva University after a three-year post-doctoral fellowship in Israel during which I undertook a transition from Judaic scholarship to Jewish education. Shortly thereafter, I noticed that the Rabbinic Alumni of Yeshiva University was planning to hold their annual mid-winter convention on the theme of "The Rav as Educator." Thinking that the topic to be explored would be the relationships between day schools and synagogue clergy, I decided to attend—although I am not a rabbinic alumnus.

It quickly became clear that "the Rav" was not your local Orthodox rabbi but "THE Rav," Rabbi Joseph B. Soloveitchik, and the panel comprised educators who had studied with him at the affiliated Rabbi Isaac Elchanan Theological Seminary (RIETS). I soon came to question my decision to attend as one rabbi after the other merely recounted how, during their tenure at the Maimonides School, Rabbi Soloveitchik had responded when asked whether they should teach this or that Tosafot or Ramban. However, I was loath to leave (probably out of embarrassment) and stuck it out. The final presentation made the wait worthwhile.

The last speaker was Rabbi Dr. Walter Wurzberger. He shared an account of a conversation he had had with the Rav when he informed his *"rebbe,"* from whom he had received *semikhah*, that he was going to Harvard to study Jewish philosophy with Professor Harry Wolfson. According to Wurzberger, the Rav, in turn, reminisced about a conversation he had had with his father, Rabbi Moses Soloveitchik, when he informed him that he was going to Berlin to study Jewish philosophy with Professor Julius Guttman.

I experienced a sudden insight: Of all the self-proclaimed *talmidim* of the Rav on that panel, the only one who had been completely true to their master's method was Wurzberger. The others had merely taken what they had heard from their teacher and enshrined it, unchanged, in their own pedagogy. Wurzberger, on the other hand, had taken the Rav's teaching as his thesis and was actively seeking an antithesis at Harvard, just as the Rav himself had sought out in Berlin an antithesis to the Torah of Brisk. There is no more reliable evidence than this of devotion to the philosophical method of synthesis that Rabbi Soloveitchik preached and practiced, and that is purported to be at the heart of Yeshiva University's motto of "Torah U'Madda"—religion and worldy knowledge.

This experience stimulated me to do something similar: I would use the Rav as a counterfoil to what I had learned through the disciplines of history and philology. Although I had not studied with Rabbi Soloveitchik personally, I have clear recollections of sitting in the balcony of YU's Lamport Auditorium during his public lectures—sometimes in the company of Pinchas Peli, the Israeli journalist and author, who sat with a stack of steno pads and faithfully rendered the Rav's words for publication in a number of Hebrew editions he subsequently issued.

I was then serving as the educational director of the nascent Torah Education Network (TEN), jointly sponsored by Yeshiva University and the Torah Education Department of the World Zionist Organization. They accepted my proposal to include essays by the Rav with my personal explications in a newly-launched pedagogical series called "Texts and Topics" that aimed to bring to high school teachers themes of modern Orthodox and religious Zionist interest and concern. "The Singularity of the Land of Israel," included in this collection, was the first fruit of that effort.

Of the manifold subjects that attracted the Rav's speculative attention and practical wisdom, prayer stood out, in my eyes, as the one most worthy of dissemination. As a result, perhaps, of his own unique upbringing at the combined hands of his father, steeped in the punctilious traditions of Brisk, his mother, who would read to him from the Russian poet and playwright Pushkin, and his *melammed* (tutor), a Lubavitch Hasid, the Rav acquired a multifaceted perspective on prayer that defies simple characterization. His own acquired linguistic and literary sensitivities further enabled him to share his insights in particularly apt and expressive terms. As a result, several of the essays included herein focus on one or another aspect of his views on prayer. But, again, they are not exclusively the Rav's thoughts on prayer, but also include my own, distilled through the filters of biblical exegesis and historical philology and refracted through his profound intuition.

Another appealing facet of the Rav was his willingness to be identified publicly with religious Zionism, including his tenure as honorary president of the Religious Zionists of America—Mizrahi HaPoel HaMizrahi. Indeed, in politically liberal modern Orthodox circles in Israel the Rav has assumed the role of halakhic and spiritual guide that in more conservative circles is held by the rabbis Kook.[1]

Several of the chapters in this book are straightforward adaptations of essays published by the Rav himself[2] or drawn from anthologies of his lectures such as those published by Rabbi Abraham Besdin.[3] These chapters should be distinguished from the remaining chapters in which I take the Rav,

1. See Yitzhak Geiger: "The New Religious Zionism" (Hebrew), *Akdamut* 11 (2001), 51-77.
2. These include: Redemption and Prayer, Fate Destiny, Spiritual Sobriety, and Heroism.
3. These include: Prayer as Dialogue, Empathy, Singularity, and Hakafot.

so to speak, to places where he himself did not go. For instance, while the Rav addressed the subject of prayer in general, he did not write specifically about Adam praying for rain, Abraham for Sodom, or the Israelites for freedom; those are my original applications of principles he articulated about prayer to those situations. The same can be said about the chapter on spirituality, in which I also apply the writings of other philosophers, including Abraham Joshua Heschel and Yeshayahu Leibowitz.

All citations from the Rav, and other authors, are footnoted; statements that are not attributed reflect my own insights. I trust that my relative unsophistication in expressing philosophical matters will be overlooked in consideration of my attempt to make the Rav's thoughts on a range of subjects better known to an audience that endeavors to harmonize its own beliefs and practices with the principles he articulated.

TECHNICALITIES

All translations of classic Jewish sources are my own, unless otherwise noted, as are the translations of material published by the Rav in Hebrew. The names of biblical characters appear in their accepted English formulations (e.g., Moses, Samuel), while those of post-biblical personalities use their standard Hebrew forms (e.g., Moshe Feinstein, the Amora Shmuel).

The following abbreviations are used in the notes throughout the book

- Abraham Besdin (ed.): "Prayer as Dialogue," in *Reflections of the Rav* (Jerusalem, 1979), 71 ff.: "Prayer"
- Joseph B. Soloveitchik: "The Lonely Man of Faith," *Tradition* 7/2 (Summer, 1965): "Lonely Man"
- Joseph B. Soloveitchik: "Redemption, Prayer, Talmud Torah," *Tradition* 17/2 (1978): "Redemption"
- Joseph B. Soloveitchik: "The Community," *Tradition* 17/2 (1978), 19-22: "Community"
- Joseph B. Soloveitchik: *Worship of the Heart* (NJ: KTAV, 2003): "Worship"
- Joseph B. Soloveitchik: *Family Redeemed* (NJ: KTAV, 2000): "Family"
- Abraham Besdin (ed.): "Reflections on Freedom and Slavery," in *Reflections of the Rav* (Jerusalem, 1979), 197 ff.: "Reflections"
- Joseph B. Soloveitchik: *"Be-Inyan Semikhat Ge'ulah Li-Tefillah,"* in *Shi'urim le-Zeikher Abba Mari Z"L* (Jerusalem, 1985): *"Shi'urim"*
- Abraham R. Besdin (ed.): "Teaching with Clarity and Empathy" in *Reflections of the Rav* (Jerusalem, 1979), 150 ff.: "Empathy"
- Joseph B. Soloveitchik: "A Tribute to the Rebbetzin of Talne," *Tradition* 17:2 (1978), 76 ff.: "Tribute"

- Joseph B. Soloveitchik: "The Future of Jewish Education in America," May 28, 1975. Cited by Aaron Rakeffet: *The Rav* (New Jersey, 1999), II: "Future"
- Abraham R. Besdin (ed.): "The Singularity of the Land of Israel," in *Reflections of the Rav* (Jerusalem, 1979), 117 ff.: "Singularity"
- Joseph B. Soloveitchik: *Fate and Destiny: From the Holocaust to the State of Israel* (NY: Ktav, 1992): "Fate and Destiny"
- Joseph B. Soloveitchik: "Towards the Metaphysical Significance of the Holiday of Purim," *Ten Da'at* 16 (2003), 69 ff.: "Metaphysical"
- Joseph B. Soloveitchik: "Catharsis," *Tradition* 17:2 (Spring 1978), 38 ff.: "Catharsis"
- Abraham Besdin (ed.): "Hakafot—Moving in Circles," in *Man of Faith in the Modern World* (KTAV, 1989), 150 ff.: "Hakafot"

THE RAV ON PRAYER

GENERAL CONSIDERATIONS[4]

PREFACE

How often have we plaintively asked one or more of the following questions:

1. Why must I pray at all?
2. Is it not presumptuous to assume that God is going to listen to me? How do I know if/when He is listening?
3. Why should I continue to pray to Him if I do not get what I pray for?
4. Why must I pray at fixed intervals and not when the mood/need strikes me?
5. How can prayer be personalized if I can only use someone else's words?

---

4. "Prayer," 71 ff.

6. Why should the presence of a *minyan* (quorum) make a difference to my personal prayers? It is unlikely that we are all praying for precisely the same thing/reason.

I shall attempt to answer some of these questions by including excerpts from several essays by the Rav. While he did not answer these questions in a systematic fashion, his writings are profoundly illuminating and stimulate considerable thought. The sources cited are open to various interpretations and, as indicated in the introduction, some of what is expressed here is my own.

INTRODUCTION: "PRAYER" IS A MISNOMER

Before we introduce the Rav's particular comments, let us begin with a quick analysis of the technical terms that many Jews colloquially call "*davening*." We customarily use the English word "prayer" as though it were entirely synonymous with the Hebrew *tefillah*.[5] A closer look at the etymologies of the two words, however, indicates that they are definitely not identical. The verb "pray" actually means "entreat"

---

5. See Moshe Sokolow: "*Rahamim* does not mean mercy; etymological scrupulousness and Torah Study" (Hebrew), in Yotam Benziman (ed.): *Leshon Rabbim: Ivrit ki-Sefat Tarbut* (Jerusalem: Van Leer Institute, 2013), 194-200.

or "beseech," and the noun "prayer" means a request or petition. In Hebrew, the corresponding verb is *le-vakkesh*, and the noun form—*bakkashah*. *Bakkashah* (or *tehinah*), as we know, is but a single aspect of *tefillah* and hardly synonymous with the entire enterprise.

Tefillah, on the other hand, derives from the verbal root *p-l-l* (hence the *dagesh* in the *lamed* of the noun *tefillah*), which has the connotation of intervention or arbitration. The noun *pelilim* (Exodus 21:22), for example, means "court," and the reflexive verbal form *le-hitpallel* means "to judge oneself." A far better English translation of *tefillah* would therefore be "introspection." While standing in self-judgment, a person might be inclined to "pray," that is, to petition God to meet a perceived need. That same person, however, might conclude that all his needs have been met, and will incline, instead, to offer God praise rather than petition. If his recent experience includes deliverance from jeopardy, he might respond to God with thanksgiving.

We "pray," then (for simplicity's sake, I will continue to use the colloquialism), for a variety of purposes, including petition, praise, and thanksgiving. Of these three categories, the one we have selected to treat here, because of its prominence, is petition. If we take the *'amidah* (*Shemoneh 'Esrei*) for example, we find that although the first three *berakhot* comprise praise and the last three thanksgiving, the core (the middle thirteen *berakhot*) of this most oft-repeated Jewish prayer consists of petitions.

THE RAV: PRAYER AS DIALOGUE

Among the questions we posed at the outset are: Why must I pray at all? How do I know if/when God is listening? Why should I continue to pray to Him if I do not get what I pray for? The Rav answered as follows:

> The very essence of prayer is the covenantal experience of being together with, and talking to, God, and that the concrete performance— such as the recitation of texts—represents the technique of implementation of prayer, and not prayer itself.[6]

The essence of prayer, according to the Rav, is a dialogue between man and God. The Rav poignantly observed:

> In prayer… we have a dialogue which is reciprocal and bilateral. Man climbs the mountain toward God while He descends, figuratively, from the mountain top. Two hands embrace, as in a handshake. "And the

---

6. "Lonely Man," 35.

Lord came down upon Mt. Sinai, on the top of the mountain; and the Lord called Moses to the top of the mountain and Moses went up" (Exodus 19:20).... In prayer both God and man move....

Prayer, we said, is a dialogue, not a monologue. A dialogue exists when one person addresses another, even if the other is temporarily silent. In prophecy, God speaks and man is silent; in prayer, there is the reverse situation. We have the assurance that He is a *shome'a tefillah* (that He hears our prayers), even if He does not accede to our wishes. He is not necessarily a *mekabbel tefillah* (responsive to our specific requests)....

In prayer we do not seek a response to a particular request as much as we desire fellowship with God. Prayer is not a means for wheedling some benefit from God. Despite our prayer: *utekabbel berahamim uberatzon et tefillatenu* (accept our prayer with compassion and pleasure), it is our persistent hope that this may be fulfilled, but it is not our primary motivation.

Our sages felt that the acceptance of our prayers is beyond our understanding and is governed by unknowable considerations. We do not really understand why some prayers are accepted and others rejected. Nevertheless, prayer in the sense of petition does play a central role in our *Shemoneh Esrei*....

Dialogue means communication, engagement, and interaction. When we pray, God emerges out of His transcendence and forms a companionship with us; the Infinite and the finite meet and the vast chasm is bridged.[7]

TEFILLAH AND "MOOD": MAIMONIDES VS. NAHMANIDES

Another of the questions we posed is: Why must I pray at fixed intervals and not when the mood/need strikes me?

The next selection from the Rav offers us an answer by means of the distinction he drew between the positions of Maimonides and Nahmanides on the origin of the mitzvah of *tefillah*.

Essentially, Maimonides and Nahmanides disagree on whether this mitzvah is of Torah origin (*de-oraita*) or of rabbinic origin (*de-rabbanan*). Maimonides regarded it as a Torah requirement, listing it in his *Sefer ha-Mitzvot* as the fifth of the 613 commandments. Nahmanides, however, considered prayer, in general, to be rabbinic; only prayer in times of collective distress is a Torah imperative. According to the Rav:

---

7. "Prayer," 77-78.

The views of Maimonides and Nahmanides can be reconciled. Both regarded prayer as meaningful only if it is derived from a sense of *tzarah*. They differ in their understanding of the word.[8]

The Rav proceeded to draw a distinction between external distress—caused by poverty, illness, or oppression—and an internal, "existential" malaise which derives from feelings of insecurity and loneliness (themes very prominent in the Rav's philosophy). This intellectual and emotional distress, the Rav claimed, provoked the Psalmist to exclaim: "From the straits I call out to God" (Psalms 118:5), and it produces the urge to pray:

Out of this sense of discomfiture prayer emerges. Offered in comfort and security, prayer is a paradox, modern methods of suburban worship and plush synagogues notwithstanding. The desire for proximity of wife and children at services comes from a need for security and comfort. Real prayer is derived from loneliness, helplessness, and a sense of dependence.[9]

8. "Prayer," 80.
9. "Prayer," 81.

The public distress (the Rav called it "surface crisis") that Nahmanides envisioned as a stimulus to prayer is the kind that comes suddenly, openly, and strikes everyone. The personal crisis (the Rav called it "depth crisis") that Maimonides viewed as sufficient cause for prayer, however, can grow gradually, clandestinely, affecting some individuals and not others. Even the most insensitive people will realize when they are in public common danger, but only the reflective and introspective will appreciate the onset of a personal crisis:

> The Torah bids man actively to combat and possibly eliminate superficial, external crises. The ills of poverty, disease, and war are debilitating and impair our spiritual freedom. The Torah, however, encourages man to embrace the experience of the "depth crisis." Thereby does man fully grasp the reality of his condition and become stirred to great heights of the spirit.[10]

The challenge of a "surface crisis" is met with solutions; a "depth crisis," on the other hand, can only be met with prayer.

---

10. "Prayer," 81

PRAYER AND PETITION IN TANAKH:
A TEMPLATE

Thus far we have established that, from a posture of introspection and self-judgment, petition is the most prominent and significant of the three principal ways in which we can relate to God. Before continuing with the Rav's analysis, however, let us turn directly to the Tanakh and explore several examples of biblical petition.[11]

1. Moses (Numbers 12:13)

The most concise petition in Tanakh is the one which Moses recited on behalf of his sister, Miriam. It consists of five words, *Kel na refa na lah,* "Please Lord, please heal her," which can be divided as follows:

(a) an address: Lord

(b) a petition: please heal her

2. Samson (Judges 16:28)

A slightly longer and more complex prayer was recited by Samson as he stood chained to the pillars in the temple of Dagon. It may be divided as follows:

(a) an address: "Lord God"

(b) a petition: "remember me and strengthen me this one time"

11. Cf. Moshe Greenberg: *Biblical Prose Prayer* (Berkeley: University of California, 1983).

(c) the supplicant's motivation: "that I may avenge [the loss of] my eyes from the Philistines"

3. Hannah (1 Samuel 1:11 ff.)

To these elements of address, petition, and motivation, Hannah's prayer for a son adds a fourth element: self-deprecation.

(a) the address: "Lord of hosts"
(b) self-deprecation: "your maidservant's distress"
(c) the actual petition: "grant your maidservant a male offspring"
(d) motivation for the petition: "I shall give him to the Lord all the days of his life"[12]

4. Jacob (Genesis 32:10-13)

The most sophisticated prayer of petition in the Bible, however, is the one that Jacob offered on the eve of his reunion with Esau. Here we have no fewer than seven separate elements (including those we have already observed):

(a) an address: "God of my father"
(b) a description of the addressee: "who instructed me to return to my homeland"

12. Hannah's petition serves in the Talmud (*Berakhot* 31a-b) as the paradigm for all Jewish prayer.

(c) a statement of self-deprecation: "I am humbled by all the graciousness"

(d) detail of self-deprecation: "I crossed the Jordan with [but] my staff, and now I number two camps"

(e) the actual petition: "spare me, please, from my brother"

(f) description of distress: "lest he come and smite me"

(g) motivation: that You may fulfill Your promise: "whereas You said 'I shall surely do well with you.'"

Additional examples include King Hezekiah (2 Kings 19:15-19) and the sailors in Jonah (1:14). Note that in each and every case we have cited from the Bible the "address," with its overtones of praise or thanksgiving, precedes the actual petition.

BAKKASHAH VS. TEHINAH: HOW DO WE APPROACH GOD IN PRAYER?

Part of our very first question is: Is it not presumptuous to assume that God is going to listen to me? In other words, is not prayer an act of "hubris" (unforgivable arrogance)? In this section, we will see that the Rav's definition of prayer offers us an important insight into the way we approach God to petition Him.

In an earlier section, we provided a philological analysis of the word *tefillah*. Here we pause to analyze a pair of technical terms: *bakkashah* and *tehinah*. The Rav noted that *bakkashah* designates a claim or a demand—something to which we feel entitled, while he defined *tehinah* (based upon the commentary of Rashi on Deut. 3:23) as something we have no reasonable expectation of receiving (*mattenat hinnam*):

> The word *tehinah* suggests an unearned grace, something not due to us.... We prefer *tehinah* to *bakashah*, because the latter suggests a claim, a demand. The principal topic of Jewish prayer is *tehinah*; praise and thanksgiving are merely prologues and epilogues.... We petition without offering any apologies; it is most legitimate, but the request is always for *mattenat hinnam*, a gift which we do not deserve.[13]

The notion of entreating God for a favor can be tied into the halakhic prescription of how He should be approached in prayer.[14] The *Shulhan Arukh* indicates

---

13. "Prayer," 84.
14. See Rabbi Saul Berman's introduction to the R.C.A. edition of the ArtScroll Siddur, entitled: "An Overview— the 'Approach' in Prayer."

that three forward steps should be taken prior to the recitation of the 'amidah (which we have already identified as being, quintessentially, a prayer of *tehinah*). The reason is not stipulated; however, the author of *Sefer Roke'ah* suggested that these paces are patterned after the three times the word *va-yiggash* ("and he approached") is utilized in the Bible: once each for Abraham, Judah, and Elijah.

ABRAHAM

When he approached God on behalf of Sodom (Genesis 18:23),[15] Abraham had no reasonable expectation of having his petition granted. God had declared Sodom an evil city and its wickedness had prompted Him to destroy it. He was already extending a courtesy to Abraham by sparing his nephew, Lot. By what right did Abraham seek to have the entire city spared? It was surely not because they deserved it.

JUDAH

When Joseph threatened to imprison Benjamin, Judah stepped forward to plead for his release (Genesis 44:18). He was so certain that his appeal would be denied that he had already volunteered to be enslaved in his brother's stead. The language he employed ("please, sir... you are just like Pharaoh") reflected his subservience to Joseph and his recognition that

---

15. See "Abraham and Sodom," below.

he was asking for something to which the second to Pharaoh would not think him entitled.

ELIJAH

Finally, when Elijah confronted the priests of Baal atop Mt. Carmel, he, too, prayed to God for success (1 Kings 18:36). However, Elijah did not merely petition God; rather, he tried, as it were, to "coerce" God into granting his request. He set up a challenge to the priests of Baal and then demanded that God back him up. From where did he derive such audacity?

Rabbi Saul Berman distinguished between these three plaintiffs based upon three considerations:

(1) By what right did each pray to God?
(2) On whose behalf did they pray?
(3) To which quality of God did they appeal?

The schematic which he included demonstrates the conclusions he drew from his investigation:

	By what right	for whom	for what quality
Abraham	as a party to a covenant (*ben berit*)	mankind	justice
Judah	as a servant	the Jewish people	mercy
Elijah	as a prophet; party to an intimate relationship with God	God Himself	revelation (God's presence)

These three examples of approaching God provide us with an answer to the question of how we engage Him with the presumption that our prayers will be answered. We see, now, that there are indeed several grounds on which to base that assumption: God is more likely to respond to a party to His covenant, to His servants, and to those with whom He enjoys a special relationship. As Psalms (99:6) records: "Like Moses and Aaron amongst His priests, and like Samuel amongst those who proclaimed His name; all call out to God who answers them."

MINYAN: THE COMPANY OF
OTHERS AND THE WORDS OF OTHERS

Two additional questions we posed at the outset deal with private vs. public prayer: What advantage does public prayer (*tefillah be-tzibbur*) have over private prayer, and why are the words of the Siddur superior to one's own?

In this final section we will try to answer these questions by means of the distinction the Rav drew between *tze'akah* and *tefillah*, two terms for prayer that appear to be used in the Bible synonymously. The Rav, however, distinguished between *tze'akah*, a cry of pain and suffering, and *tefillah*, the articulation of need.

Using the Israelite slavery in Egypt as the paradigm of suffering and the Exodus as the model of redemption,[16] the Rav drew a lesson in prayer from the story of Moses.

What is the connection, he asked, between the episodes in which Moses protected a Jewish slave and interceded to stop a quarrel (Exodus 2:11 ff.) and the statement that follows (v. 23): "And it came to pass in the course of many days... that the Children of Israel sighed on account of their bondage and they cried out..."? The *Zohar*'s explanation, expanded by the Rav, is that in the state of slavery the Jews were mute, incapable of sound, let alone articulate speech. They knew pain—in the physical sense—but not suffering, which is not a physical sensation, but a spiritual experience. They thought their condition was normative and only after Moses demonstrated to them that they were the victims of injustice did their sensitivity return, and, with it, their ability to cry out.

The ability to cry out to God is the prelude to prayer but not yet prayer itself. Crying out reflects an awareness of pain, the yearning of the sufferer for relief, but it does not yet recognize what the Rav called "a hierarchy of needs." To cry out to God is to release pent up emotions almost arbitrarily; to pray to God is to have reflected on a variety of needs and to prioritize one's requests intelligently.

---

16. See "Slavery and Redemption" below.

Judaism... wants man to cry out aloud against any kind of pain, to react indignantly to all kinds of injustice or unfairness.... Whoever permits his legitimate needs to go unsatisfied will never be sympathetic to the crying needs of others.... For Judaism, need-awareness constitutes part of the definition of human existence....

Prayer is the doctrine of human needs. Prayer tells the individual, as well as the community, what his, or its, genuine needs are, what he should, or should not, petition God about.... In short, through prayer man finds himself. Of course, the very instant he finds himself, he becomes a redeemed being.[17]

Man cannot pray for others until he has prayed for himself. The converse, too, holds true: Man cannot pray for himself without including others in his prayers. Once he recognizes his responsibility to pray for others, the Rav said, the supplicant has created "a community of prayer."

What does this mean? It means a community of common pain, of common suffering. The Halacha has taught the individual to include his fellow man in his prayer. The individual

17. "Redemption," 65-66.

must not limit himself to his own needs, no matter how pressing those needs are and how distinguished he is. Halacha has formulated prayer in the plural.... Even private prayers, such as those offered on the occasion of sickness, death, or other crises, are recited in the plural....

Knesset Yisrael is a prayerful community, in which every individual experiences not only his own pain, but also that of countless others. I still remember the distress we young boys experienced when we heard of a pogrom in some Jewish town thousands of miles away. Our anguish was not due to fear, but to sympathy and compassion. We felt the pain of the nation as a whole.[18]

Halakhah prescribes communal prayer (*tefillah be-tzibbur*) as an antidote to man's existential loneliness, but loneliness is but one of the two sides of man's slavish existence; the other is his ignorance:

When I say that man is ignorant, I do not refer to his scientific achievements; in this area modern man is clever and ingenious. What man fails to comprehend is not the world around him, but the world within him,

18. "Community," 19-22.

particularly his destiny, and the needs of which he is supposed to have a clear awareness.... Because of this misidentification, man adopts the wrong table of needs which he feels he must gratify. Man responds quickly to the pressure of certain needs, not knowing *whose* needs he is out to gratify.

At this juncture, sin is born. What is the cause of sin if not the diabolical habit of man to be mistaken about his own self? ... Does the young man understand his basic needs? If he did, we would have no problem of crime, drugs and permissiveness in general.... Modern man is, indeed, existentially a slave, because he is ignorant and fails to identify his own needs.[19]

Just as the presence of others praying alleviates the loneliness of man's existence, the use of liturgical formulas relieves him of the burden of identifying his needs and making proper petition to have them met. Instead of leaving man to blunder in the maze of real or presumed needs, *halakhah* canonized them and requires him only to recite them. (There is license, however, to insert individualized requests in the blessing of *shome'a tefillah*.)

---

19. "Redemption," 61-63.

IN REVIEW AND CONCLUSION
Here, again, are the questions with which we began, and a synopsis of the answers we have provided, based upon our premises that: (a) conceptually, prayer is a form of arbitration and self-judgment; yet, (b) normative, operative, prayer is petition.

1. Why must I pray at all?
Since petitionary prayer stems from the recognition of need, an intelligent, introspective person imposes the obligation to pray upon himself. The ability to pray, i.e., to engage in spontaneous "needs-awareness," is one of the distinguishing characteristics of a free and sentient being.

2. Is it not presumptuous to assume that God is going to listen to me? How do I know if/when He is listening?
By virtue of either (a) the covenantal relationship (modeled by Abraham), (b) the master-servant relationship (Judah), or (c) the intimate, *ben-bayit*, relationship (Elijah), we have the right and confidence with which to approach God at all times, even for what amounts to a favor we have no right to expect (*mattenat hinnam*).

3. Why should I continue to pray to Him if I do not get what I pray for?

If we are committed to prayer as dialogue, we should continue to speak to God even in the face of His apparent silence. He offers us no guarantee that He will accept our prayers/petitions, only that He will listen.[20]

4. Why must I pray at fixed intervals and not when the mood/need strikes me?

The disagreement between Maimonides and Nahmanides offers an insight into the establishment of fixed intervals for prayer. Note that Maimonides understood prayer as a response to personal need, rather than public danger, coupled with the understanding that greater sensitivity is required for prayer than for just crying out. Thus, if there were no fixed prayers, we would be at risk of failing to pray at all!

5. How can prayer be personalized if one can only use someone else's words?

---

20. When kidnapped Nahshon Wachsman, הי"ד, was murdered in 1994, his father, Yehudah Wachsman, was asked whether his belief in God had been shaken by the fact that God had denied his prayers, and the prayers of so many other people, to spare his son. His answer was: לאבא מותר גם לומר לא; a father is also entitled to say "no."

The Rav invited us to understand that it is man's essential ignorance that leads to his misidentification of his own needs, and, ultimately, to sin. Were man left entirely to his own petitionary designs, he might never make the proper requests of God. The formulaic pattern of the 'amidah, for instance, insures that some of man's real needs are addressed regularly.

6. Why should the presence of a *minyan* make a difference to my personal prayers? It is unlikely that we are all praying for the same thing/reason.
The Rav cited man's essential loneliness, along with his ignorance, as the principal problems of human existence. The presence of a quorum in prayer is an invitation to man to overcome his loneliness, albeit temporarily. By joining with others in prayer—even by praying alone yet in the grammatical plural—man creates "community."

ADAM AND THE RAIN

THE FIRST "NEEDS ASSESSMENT"

PREFACE

The Rav's quintessential definition of *tefillah* is "to ask intelligently,"[21] or, as he also defined it, to conduct an accurate needs assessment. He also addressed the singular importance of "petitionary" prayer (*bakkashah*), saying: "Petition is the main form of human prayer,"[22] "even two of the last three benedictions [*retzeh* and *sim shalom*] are of a petitional nature."[23]

In this section, we shall examine the case of a petition that was offered in absentia, as it were; a prayer whose very existence can only be inferred from

---

21. "Redemption," 67. In "The Rav on Prayer" above, I defined *tefillah* as introspection.
22. "Worship," 10-11, 28ff.
23. "Redemption," 65.

the Torah text, and which, nevertheless, demonstrates an indispensable principle of the prayer relationship between Man and God.

RESOLVING A CONTRADICTION

1. In Genesis 1:12, the Torah states: "The earth brought forth vegetation…" indicating that grass had begun to grow on day three of creation.

2. In Genesis 2:5, however, we read: "No shrub of the field [si'ah ha-sadeh] had yet appeared in the earth, neither had any herb of the field begun to grow, because the Lord God had not caused rain to fall on the earth and there was no human to cultivate it." This implies that there was no vegetation—because there was no precipitation—prior to the creation of man on day six.

3. BT *Hullin* 60b states:

This indicates that the vegetation was held at the earth's surface until Adam came and prayed for it; then the rains came, and it grew.

In other words, R. Assi resolved this contradiction by positing that the vegetation was kept poised just below the surface of the earth from day three until day six, when Adam came and recited a prayer for rain. From this resolution, R. Assi then inferred a momentous theological postulate: "God craves the prayer of the righteous."[24]

SOME THOUGHTS ABOUT
THE MUTUALITY OF PRAYER

In Numbers 28:2, in regard to the "regular offerings" (*korban tamid*), God put us in charge of what He called: "MY near-offerings [*korbani*], MY food [*lahmi*], MY fire-offerings ([*le'ishai*], MY soothing savor [*rei'ah nihohi*]" (translations follow Everett Fox).

This permits—or, perhaps, even mandates—the following syllogism:

1. Sacrifices are God's food (as it were), and He is dependent on us for His satisfaction.
2. Prayer is the substitute for sacrifice.
3. Therefore, just as He previously depended upon our regular sacrifices, He now depends upon our regular prayer.

Our prayer, then, is decidedly not a one-sided affair in which we beseech God for unmerited divine assistance, favor, or grace. On the contrary, it is part of a pact, a covenant if you will, between parties

---

24. This interpretation is based upon the homiletical stipulation of the Sages that *sihah*, as in *si'ah ha-sadeh* (Gen. 2:5), also means prayer (*Berakhot* 26b).

who, however unequal in capacity, are nonetheless mutually dependent.[25]

CONNECTING PRAYER AND *PARNASAH*

Regarding the association of prayer with sacrifice just noted, Rabbi Naftali Tzvi Yehudah Berlin (Netziv, 1817-1893) observed:

> This is the difference between all *mitzvot* of the Torah and sacrifices or prayer. All the other *mitzvot* and forms of worship either have their rewards withheld until the world to come, or their benefits are reaped directly in this world—in wealth and honor and the like, a *quid pro quo* [*middah keneged middah*].
>
> Sacrifices and prayer, on the other hand, are essentially [performed] in order to sustain essential livelihood. To wit: "[Why is the altar called] *mizbe'ah*? Because it is *meizin* [provides sustenance]" (*Ketubot* 10b).
>
> Established prayer [*tefillah kevu'ah*] is similarly referred to as "temporal life" [*hayyei sha'ah*] and all the blessings over pleasure [*birkhot ha-nehenin*] are likewise meant to bless the abundance of that species.
>
> We note in *Berakhot* (35a) that taking pleasure in this world without reciting a

---

blessing is comparable to stealing from God and the community of Israel, to wit: "One who steals from his father or mother saying, 'It is no crime,' is akin to a man of destruction" (Proverbs 18:9), such as Jeroboam son of Nebat who destroyed [the relationship] between Israel and its heavenly Father.

The meaning behind this is as follows: The blessings over pleasure cause the abundance of that species and whoever withholds these blessings is stealing from God, Who wishes to provide the abundance, and from the community of Israel, which is in need of it. He is akin to Jeroboam who [by erecting the golden calves] prevented Israel from bringing the sacrifices that stimulate blessing.[26]

SOME HALAKHIC DIMENSIONS

Ordinarily, the nature of petition restricts its recitation to weekdays; hence, the elimination of the intermediate *berakhot* from the *'amidah* of Shabbat and Yom Tov. The same principle appears to govern the similar restriction against the recitation, on Shabbat, of *Avinu Malkenu*:

It is customary to recite *Avinu Malkenu* in its proper place. If it is Shabbat, however, it

---

26. *Ha'amek Davar* to Genesis 2:5.

is not recited (*Orah Hayyim* 584). The reason is that we do not recite petitionary prayers on Shabbat (*Mishnah Berurah*, ad. loc.).

R. Shlomo Zalman Auerbach drew a fine distinction—one that is in tune with the Rav's differentiation between prayer and crying-out—with regard to other forms of existential "needs assessments":

Q: Why, then, is it permissible to recite petitions on Rosh Hashanah when it is equally inappropriate to experience distress?

A: It is permissible to "sound the alarm" on Shabbat. It is permissible to pray on account of great [public] distress even on Shabbat. On Rosh Hashanah, the Day of Judgment, on which we are all in great distress, it is thus permissible to petition.[27]

The *Mishnah Berurah* found similar grounds to permit the recitation on Shabbat of prayers that appear to be petitionary:

Others have written that it is permissible on Shabbat to recite *elokai ad shelo notzarti*, or *yehi ratzon*, because the only petition

27. Nahum Stepansky (ed.): *Ve'alehu Lo Yibbol* (Jerusalem, 1999), vol. I, 351.

that is prohibited is on account of illness or livelihood, where there is evident distress. It is appropriate, however, to express remorse daily, since it is not, strictly speaking, a "confession" (*Orah Hayyim* 288).

EXTRACTING THE SIGNIFICANCE

Reducing these propositions to more existential terms, it places man—rather than the earth—at the focus of creation and indicates that God's principal purpose in creation was not the earth itself but the earth-dweller. Man, for his part, was not intended to emerge upon the background of a completed and perfect world, but to be co-opted into partnering with God in its completion and perfection. God, therefore, did not merely provide Adam with the opportunity, or even just the incentive, to pray for the rain that would complete creation; He positively yearned for human prayer without which His own plan and intent would have been frustrated.

The consequences of this realization are exceedingly far-reaching. As much as we are dependent upon God and His grace, so is He dependent upon our participation in His worldly enterprise. This would appear to give us considerable leverage in our dealings with Him.[28]

---

28. See "Abraham at Sodom," below.

ABRAHAM AND SODOM:

PETITION, INTERCESSION, AND "DIVINE INTIMACY"

PREFACE

The Rav wrote:

> [Prayer] consists of both experiencing the complete helplessness of man, his absolute dependence upon God, and the performance of the ritual of prayer, of reciting fixed texts.[29]
>
> Does *avodah she-ba-lev* exhaust itself in standardized action, in the recital of a fixed text thrice daily, or in an inner experiential reality, in spiritual activity? ... The physical deed of reciting a fixed text serves only as a medium through which the experience finds

---

29. Joseph B. Soloveitchik: *Family Redeemed* (NJ: KTAV, 2000), 40.

its objectification and concretion. It is not to
be identified with the genuine act of praying,
which is to be found in an entirely different
dimension, namely, in the great, wondrous
God-experience.[30]

The example of Abraham at Sodom illustrates yet
another principle of prayer: the integration of petition
(*bakkashah*) into the set liturgical order. Abraham,
the first of the Patriarchs (*avot*), is cited in the Torah
several times as "calling out in God's name" (e.g.,
Genesis 12:8), ostensibly, an early form of prayer.

So accomplished did Abraham become at prayer,
that he was seen as a paradigm of intercessory prayer
in his own lifetime. After chastising the Philistines on
account of Sarah, God advised Abimelech to "return
the man's wife; indeed, he is a prophet and can
intercede on your behalf and you will live" (Genesis
20:7). In fact, turning to a righteous person to assist
through prayer in time of need is an enduring Jewish
practice.

Recognition of the *avot* as paradigms of prayer
may also account for the halakhic ruling that
kavvanah, intentionality,[31] is required only for the
first blessing of the 'amidah, known as *birkhat avot*.

---

30. "Worship," 19-20.
31. On *kavvanah*, per se, see the closing section of *Tefillot:
Avot Tikkenum*, below.

WHY TELL?

In Genesis 18, God was about to destroy the cities of Sodom and Gomorrah on account of their great iniquity and the cry that had ascended to Him. At what appeared to be the last moment, He recalled that He was not supposed to launch such a catastrophe without providing prior notice to His servant, Abraham: "Am I going to hide from Abraham what I am about to do?" (18:17). Given this information, Abraham proceeded to remonstrate with God, praying and pleading on behalf of Sodom. The question, of course, is: Did God expect Abraham to respond otherwise? If it was His intention to destroy the cities, why open the matter for negotiation?

In fact, the same question can be asked of any of a number of instances reported in Tanakh in which God informed people of their own or others' fate, only to have them argue with Him over His decision and attempt to intercede with Him on behalf of the intended victims. (Moses, Samuel, Isaiah, and Jonah come quickly to mind.) It is as though God did not really want to carry out His verdict and He was looking to be talked out of it.

THE PARADOX OF PROPHECY

In the specific case of the prophet, however, this partnership has a paradoxical outcome. The prophet, who is—at first—the medium for the transmission of the divine threat of punishment for transgression,

becomes—in the continuation—an advocate for the
defendant before the Chief Justice, interceding in
order to have the sentence mitigated.

The fulfillment of this function inspired what
Yohanan Muffs called "prophetic intercessory
prayer":

> Prophetic prayer is the most characteristic
> indication of the prophet's total intellectual
> independence and freedom of conscience. The
> divine strong hand does not lobotomize the
> prophet's moral and emotional personality.
> Prophecy does not tolerate prophets who lack
> heart, who are emotionally anaesthetized.
> Quite the contrary, one could even argue that,
> historically speaking, the role of intercessor is
> older than the messenger aspect of prophecy.
> After all, Abraham is not a prophetic
> messenger, yet he is considered a prophet
> nonetheless. His prophetic nature manifests
> itself only in his prayer… [Gen. 20:7]. There is
> no better example of prayer and petition than
> that of Abraham in the case of Sodom, which
> distinguishes itself in its unbridled audacity
> against heaven: "Shall the Judge of the world
> not do justice?" (Gen. 18:25).[32]

32. Yohanan Muffs: "Who will stand in the breach? A
study in prophetic intercession," Idem: *Love and Joy* (NY:
JTSA, 1992), 11.

PRECEDENT

This curious, counterintuitive situation has a precedent. In "Adam and the Rain" (above), we stipulated that man is God's partner in creation. Before man prayed for rain, there was no vegetation apparent; hence, without man's active and consensual participation, creation is incomplete.

Man's responsibility to assist God to realize the full potential of creation did not end with his expulsion from the Garden of Eden; it continues, undiminished, throughout history and is ongoing today.

THE RIGHT APPROACH

Abraham's intercession at Sodom is a paradigm of yet another feature associated with prayer: the right way to approach God. When the impending fate of Sodom is first revealed to him, the Torah describes his approach to God using the word *va-yiggash*, literally, "and he came near." The *Roke'ah* (R. Eliezer ben Yehudah; c. 1165–c. 1230), as noted earlier, observed that the same word is used to describe the approaches made by two other biblical figures prior to their own acts of intercession: Judah (Genesis 44:18) and Elijah (1 Kings 18:36), and concluded that the combination of all three is the source of the three steps forward we customarily take before the *'amidah*.[33]

---

33. See: "The Rav on Prayer" above

PETITION AND REGULAR PRAYER

As the three messengers leave Abraham and turn towards Sodom, the Torah describes Abraham as: "still standing [*'omed*] before God" (Genesis 18:22). Targum Onkelos rendered the word *'omed* as: *meshamesh bi-tzlo*, "engaged in prayer."

- In what kind of prayer was Abraham already engaged, i.e., prior to God's revelation to him of the fate of Sodom?
- What is the relationship between this preexisting prayer and the petition on behalf of Sodom that followed?

The answer is given by the Netziv: "This was his fixed prayer." Only in the following verse (23) did he begin to pray specifically for Sodom, as it says, *va-yiggash Avraham*. The Netziv elaborated:

The Torah informs us about all these details to teach us that one should pray for something only as part of his regular prayer, since that is the most propitious time. As the Talmud records (*Avodah Zarah* 7b): "When does the verse apply: 'A prayer of a lowly man when he is faint'? When 'He pours forth his plea [*siho*] before God'" (Psalm 102:1). That is to say, during regular prayer, which is called a "plea" [*si'ah*].... For this reason, Abraham did not have to preface his prayer [for Sodom] with praise [of God] as the law requires, since he was already engaged in regular prayer, which contains praise.[34]

PETITION WITHIN PRAYER:
A HALAKHIC DIMENSION

The relationship of petition (*bakkashah/tehinah*) to prayer[35] is a subject of intricate halakhic inquiry by the Rav, who asked, rhetorically:

How can man—short-lived and anxiety-ridden—approach the King in petition and supplication? The entire matter of prayer is a gift of a gracious God to mortal man.... [Therefore,] it is forbidden to cry out to God without utilizing the form and framework of prayer.[36]

---

34. See הרחב דבר ad. loc. The Netziv contrasted Abraham's petition on behalf of Sodom with Jacob's petition on his own behalf (Genesis 32:10ff.), noting that since Jacob was not otherwise engaged in prayer, his petition had to commence with praise of God. See *Tefillot Avot Tikkenum* (Part Three) below, which deals with Jacob's petition in greater detail.
35. See the chapter on the nexus between redemption and prayer (below).
36. *Shi'urim*, 42.

Citing the statement of R. Simlai: "One should always arrange his praise of God [first] and afterwards he may pray" (*Avodah Zarah* 7b), the Rav stipulated two points about *tefillah*:

(a) There is an obligation to pray; one is obliged to pray and gratify his Creator, and place his petition before him.

(b) One may not petition for his needs outside of the framework of [fixed] prayer.

By inserting his petition for Sodom into the context of his regular [fixed] prayer, Abraham serves as a paradigm of this principle.

TEFILLOT—AVOT TIKKENUM

CHARACTERIZING OUR PRAYERS

PREFACE

The Rav acknowledged that the prayers of the three Patriarchs were the "historical precedent" on which the Men of the Great Assembly based traditional prayer. He wrote:

> We find that our forefathers, Moses and the prophets prostrated themselves before God in prayer, spoke with Him conversationally, revealed to Him their innermost secrets and forced Him as it were, to meet their needs, argued and demanded.[37]
>
> The fact that we commence the recital of the "eighteen benedictions" by addressing ourselves to the G-d of Abraham, Isaac

---

37. Joseph B. Soloveitchik, *"Ra'oynot al ha-Tefillah."* *Areset* 5 (Tammuz 5745), p. 254 (Hebrew).

and Jacob, is indicative of the covenantal relationship which, in the opinion of our sages, lies at the very root of prayer.[38]

CONFORMITY AND INDIVIDUALITY

While we have a tendency to speak of the three Patriarchs (*avot*) as though they were interchangeable, the truth is that with all the similarities in their actions and reactions, each possessed distinctive traits of character and personality. Each of those traits, in turn, has become identified with the Jewish people, as a collective entity, giving palpable proof to what Nahmanides called: *ma'aseh avot siman la-banim*— ancestral deeds set an example for their descendants.

The two statements that follow capture the essence of their similarities and differences in a manner particularly well-suited for understanding *tefillah*.

Berakhot 26b	*Pesahim* 88a
Abraham established *shaharit*	Abraham appeared on a mountain
Isaac established *minhah*	Isaac appeared in a field
Jacob established *'arvit*	Jacob appeared in a house

What did the Sages intend to convey via these associations?

38. "Lonely Man," 35.

THE CHARACTERIZATIONS

Abraham was called *'ivri* (Hebrew) because he had the capacity to confront his idolatrous environment with his belief in one God.[39] The light this sheds on true faith and belief is represented by the *shaharit* prayer and the standard he set for others to follow is represented by a mountain, which is visible even at a distance. Abraham's conduct both in his emigration to God's Promised Land, as well as his itinerary after his arrival, are models of devotion to the cause of monotheism and its dissemination. In other words:

> Abraham expresses the historical chapter in which the people of Israel bear God's name throughout the world and the gentile nations relate to them as a 'divine prince' in their midst. [40]

Isaac represents continuity. He strengthened the structure that Abraham erected thereby insuring that it would not be just a passing phase. Even the wells that he dug were given the same names that had been conferred on them by Abraham. Since his lot was not one of innovation, Isaac often appears passive—as in the case of the *Akeidah*, and in the arrangement of

---

39. In Hebrew, the verbal root עב"ר connotes opposition.
40. Cf. Herzog Teachers' College: *Teachers' Guide to Bereishit-Shemot* (5758), p. 27.

his marriage to Rebecca. This passivity/continuity is represented by the *minhah* prayer, which is recited at twilight—a time that is neither entirely day nor night—and by the field, which represents something at once both stable and unyielding.

> Isaac expresses the humdrum chapters in national life; the periods in which the people resided in its land, living according to the heritage of its fathers.[41]

Jacob's life, from birth and on, is characterized by struggle; hence, the attribution to him of *'arvit*, the prayer that is recited only by night—in darkness. He succeeded, however, by drawing clear lines of demarcation that kept his restless family intact. Whereas Abraham and Isaac are represented by a mountain and a field—symbolic of expansiveness— Jacob's symbol is the house; enclosed and, perhaps, even restrictive.

> Jacob's life spans the dark periods of national exile. The gathering within the house is the necessary result of the ongoing emergency that characterizes Jacob's life.[42]

---

41. *Teachers' Guide.*
42. *Teachers' Guide.*

MODELS OF PETITION

As Jacob is about to be reunited with Esau, he addressed God with an urgent plea to be delivered from what he described as impending doom and destruction. This prayer (Genesis 32:10-13), which serves as a model of what Moshe Greenberg has called "Biblical Prose Prayer,"[43] is the only such model to contain all seven of the elements we have come to expect of petition: address, description (of addressee), self-deprecation, detail (thereof), petition, distress, and motivation.

In "Abraham and Sodom," we presented the Netziv's explanation that Abraham did not need to begin his petition with praise of God because he was already engaged in regular (fixed) prayer. Jacob, on the other hand, had to begin his petition by praising God because he was not otherwise engaged in prayer. Abraham entertained his guests at noon (Gen. 18:1) and they arrived at Sodom in the evening (Gen. 19:1), therefore his plea to God—which followed his parting company with his guests—would have been in the afternoon; hence, the assumption that he would have been reciting *minhah*.

Jacob, on the other hand, had spent the day making frantic preparations for his encounter with Esau and subsequently he went to sleep (Gen. 32:14). Since he would already have recited *minhah* and

---

43. See "The Rav on Prayer" above.

apparently felt he could not delay his petition until the next regular prayer time (*'arvit*) arrived, his petition to God required an introduction.

ANOTHER COMPARISON

There are additional similarities and differences among the *avot* than those we contrasted above. For example, Abraham's stance before God is referred to as *'amidah* ("rising up," Gen. 19:27), Isaac's is called *sihah* ("conversation, discussion," 24:63), and Jacob's is *pegi'ah* ("encounter," 28:11).

As expounded by Rabbi Avi Weiss, these three verbs signify three distinct actions that may also characterize our *tefillah*.

> As one rises up, it is important to remove all the clutter, all the disturbances that could impede one's ability to communicate with God.... In conversation, one must obviously comprehend the contents of his/her words... [and] it is important to feel God's presence.[44]

The last two elements, comprehending the prayers and feeling God's presence, are the twin pillars of the Rav's definition of intentionality (*kavvanah*). Based upon a distinction first drawn by R. Hayyim Brisker, *kavvanah* is said to comprise the understanding of

44. Idem: *A Taste of Torah* (5759), Va-yetze.

the liturgy coupled with the awareness that one is standing in the presence of divinity:

תרי גווני כוונות יש בתפילה. האחת כוונה של פירוש הדברים, ויסודה הוא דין כוונה. ושנית, שיכוון שהוא עומד בתפילה לפני ה'.

There are two dimensions to intentionality in prayer. One is to have in mind the meaning of the words, and this is fundamental to intentionality. The second is to be aware that one is standing in prayer before God.[45]

---

45. *חידושי ר' חיים הלוי על הרמב"ם* (הלכות תפילה פרק ד, הלכה א).

SLAVERY AND REDEMPTION:

PRAYER AS PREREQUISITE FOR FREEDOM[46]

The very essence of prayer is the covenantal experience of being together with and talking to God and that the concrete performance, such as the recitation of texts, represents the technique of implementation of prayer and not prayer itself.[47]

PREFACE

According to the Rav, slavery is characterized by silence. Since slaves have only biological needs (as opposed to "human" ones), they may cry out, but they

---

46. Based on Joseph B. Soloveitchik: "Redemption, Prayer, Talmud Torah," *Tradition* 17/2 (Spring, 1978), 55-72; Idem: "Reflections on Freedom and Slavery," in Abraham Besdin (ed.): *Reflections of the Rav* (Jerusalem, 1979), 197-206.
47. "Lonely Man," 35.

do not pray. However, only when they find their voice in prayer can they be redeemed. The Jews in Egypt were rendered speechless by their oppression,[48] and the process of their redemption was consequently impeded.

Indeed, the Rav identified the oft-repeated mitzvah of reciting the narrative of the Exodus (*sippur yetzi'at mitzrayim*) as a paradigm of the relationship between speech and redemption. This association served several purposes for the Rav, among them the distinction between prayer (*tefillah*) and crying out (*ze'akah*) that plays a significant role in his support for Maimonides's position on the Torah origin of prayer as opposed to Nahmanides, who views it as rabbinic.[49]

In this chapter, this principle is applied to the narrative of the enslavement and oppression in Egypt at the beginning of the Book of Exodus, illustrating how an understanding of that episode can help lay the foundation for the Rav's concept of prayer.

DEFINING SLAVERY

The Rav distinguished between two aspects of slavery. He called the one "juridic" and the other "typological."

48. The Rav made a similar point about the experience of Holocaust survivors: "Former inmates of concentration camps have told me that they had, with the passage of time, become inured to any pain or torture, as if they had been totally anesthetized. They not only stopped speaking, but ceased to emit coherent sounds, as well" (*"Redemption,"* 57).
49. See "The Rav on Prayer" (*"Tefillah* and Mood") above.

The juridic aspect is the political condition in which some people—their bodies, their skills, their work product—are considered to be the property of others who may do with them as they wish, whereas the typological is "a mental state of servility... an emotional condition,"[50] a mentality that can be found even among people who are politically free. The Rav saw this distinction embodied in a passage from the Haggadah in which we offer a blessing to God "on account of our redemption (*al ge'ulateinu*) and on account of the liberation of our souls (*ve'al pedut nafsheinu*)." He identified the former as the release from juridic slavery and the latter as freedom from typological slavery.

According to *halakhah*, the slave mentality (rather than the political status) mandates that slaves be exempt from three categories of religious obligations:

- testifying in court
- positive time-bound *mitzvot*
- marriage

The common denominator among these three categories, according to the Rav, is that they require an exercise of free will of which the slave is incapable on account of his subjugation to another. The

---

50. "Reflections," 197-8.

slave's inability to make his own choices impairs his judgment, distorts his conception of truth, and reduces him to a "perpetual state of intimidation." He cannot offer testimony as it requires judgment, he cannot perform time-bound *mitzvot* "because he lacks time consciousness," and he may not marry because one who lacks free agency cannot "relate to another in a free reciprocity."

> To summarize our analysis of slavery: we indicated that the slave is a frightened personality whose truth-discernment is impaired; he is insensitive to time and is also incapable of establishing relationships.[51]

A BRIEF COMPARISON OF SLAVERIES

Our own observations of slavery and oppression from history and literature (e.g., *Uncle Tom's Cabin*, *The Gulag Archipelago*) make us aware of the common denominators of the slave experience. These observations can be compared and contrasted with those of Exodus 1:13-14, etc., and with *midreshei aggadah* on the subject. Particular attention should be paid to the several interpretations of "backbreaking work" (*'avodat perekh*)[52] and to the reappearance of

---

51. "Reflections," 203.
52. E.g., Rashi (Lev. 25:43) interpreted it as: "unnecessary work intended to subjugate him." Ibn Ezra preferred the more literal reading of Targum: "severely" (*be-kashyu*). We

perekh in the laws of Israelite servitude: Leviticus 25:43, 46, and 53 prohibit a Jewish master from imposing *perekh* work on a Jewish servant.[53]

As per American tradition, Benjamin Franklin saw a symbolic parallel between the Israelite redemption from Egypt and the American independence from England. He recommended that the Great Seal of the United States feature Moses overseeing the crossing of the Red Sea and the Egyptians drowning therein, as seen here:

---

have translated it as "backbreaking" based on the meaning of the cognate root *p-r-k* in Aramaic: to break (or crush).

53. In this spirit, Maimonides ruled that anyone who exhibits characteristics of cruelty and inhumanity towards a fellow Jew is suspect of being a descendant of the Gibeonites because a genuine Israelite is compassionate and humane (*Hilkhot Issurei Bi'ah* 19:17).

Furthermore, the similarities between the
experiences of Afro-American slavery and Israelite
slavery have been explored in detail by Kenneth
Chelst: *Exodus and Emancipation* (Jerusalem: Urim,
2009),[54] who provides several examples of how the
former identified with the fortunes of the latter:

But when Moses wif his powah/ Comes an'
sets us chillun free/ We will praise de gracious
Mastah/ Dat has gin us liberty; An' we'll shout
ouah halleluyahs,/ On dat mighty reck'nin'
day,/ When we'se reco'nized ez citiz' —Huh
uh! Chillun, let us pray![55]

Chelst also cites the following example:

One day he was out minding his father-in-
law's sheep, and the Lord spoke to Moses and
said, "Pull off your shoes, for you is on holy
ground. I want you to go back and deliver my
children from Egypt." He said, "Moses, what
is that you got in your hand?" Moses said, "It's

---

54. Also cf. Michael Walzer: *Exodus and Revolution*
(NY, 1985), who illustrated how the story of the Israelite
oppression and the Exodus has been transformed into a
symbol of political redemption, liberation, and revolution.
Notably, his introduction documents his indebtedness to
the published *Studies* of Nehama Leibowitz.
55. Laurence Dunbar (1872-1906), an Afro-American
poet: "An Ante-Bellum Sermon."

a staff." He said, "Cast it on the ground." And it turned to a snake. And Moses fled from it. The Lord said, "Go back and pick it up." And Moses picked it up, and it turned back into a staff. The Lord said, "Go back and wrought all these miracles in Egypt and deliver my children from bondage." So Moses goes on back. He goes into to Pharaoh and told him what the Lord had told him to do. Pharaoh said, "Who is he?" "I can show you what He got power to do." And he cast his rod on the floor, and it turned into a serpent. Pharaoh said, "That ain't nothing. I got a magic can do that." So he brought his magicians and soothsayers in, and they cast their rods on the floor. So theirs turned to snakes. And they crawled up to Moses' snake, and Moses' snake swallowed up their snakes. And that's where hoodoo lost its hand, because theirs was evil power and his was good. They lost their rods and he had his and theirs too.[56]

CRYING OUT VS. PRAYING

Let us next look through the early narrative of Exodus for the appearance of verbs that denote the articulation of sound.

---

56. Richard M. Dorson: *American Negro Folktales* (Greenwich, CT: Fawcett, 1967), 256-7.

- "After the passage of some time, the king of Egypt died and the Children of Israel groaned [*va-ye'anhu*] on account of their labors and they cried out [*va-yiz'aku*], and their pleas [*shav'atam*] ascended to God on account of their labors" (2:23),
- "God heard their moaning [*na'akatam*] and He recalled the covenant..." (2:24),
- "God spoke to Moses, saying... I have also heard the moaning [*na'akat*] of the Children of Israel who are enslaved by the Egyptians and I have recalled my covenant" (6:2, 5).

We can distinguish, here, between those verbs that indicate only the expression of misery (*n-'-k, '-n-h*) and other verbs that signify calling out, as in prayer (*z-'-k, sh-v-'*). We may then conclude, along with the Rav, citing the *Zohar*: "When Moses came, Voice appeared" (*ata Moshe, ata qol*);[57] namely, that the appearance of Moses and the hope that he symbolized enabled the slaves to find their voice, pray to God, and secure the promised redemption.

According to the Rav, Exodus 2:23 indicates that prior to the arrival of Moses on the scene the Jews

---

57. *Zohar*, "*Ra'ya Mehemna,*" *Va'era*. Cited in full in "Redemption," 58.

had not prayed to God because they lacked "needs awareness," a prerequisite for both liberty and prayer. However, the protest that Moses lodged with Pharaoh over their treatment, albeit initially unsuccessful, heightened their sensitivity to their own needs:

> Prayer is warranted and meaningful only when one realizes that all hope is gone, that there is no other friend besides God from whom one may expect assistance and comfort, when the soul feels its bleak despair, loneliness and helplessness.... Prayer as a personal experience, as a creative gesture, is possible only if and when man discovers himself in crisis or in need.[58]

REDEMPTION AND *TZITZIT*

The Rav also treated the theme of slavery and redemption in an unexpected context: the mitzvah of *tzitzit*.

According to the Talmud (*Shabbat* 57b), the Israelite slaves in Egypt wore an insignia, called a chain of slavery (*kavla de-avda*), which indicated their political status.[59] When they were redeemed,

---

58. David Shatz, Joel Wolowelsky, Reuven Ziegler (eds.): *Out of the Whirlwind: Essays on Mourning, Suffering, and the Human Condition* (New Jersey, 2003), 161.
59. Rashi, ad loc., defined it as "a seal worn by a slave on

they exchanged those insignias for *tzitzit*, signifying the replacement of their political masters with their spiritual Master. As God declared, apropos of the laws of Jewish servitude: "For the Children of Israel are slaves to me; they are my servants whom I did extricate from Egypt. I am the Lord your God" (Lev. 25:55). And as the Talmud interpreted that verse: "They are My slaves; they are not slaves to [other] slaves" (*Bava Kamma* 116b). This distinction also accounts for the otherwise gratuitous reference, within the Torah's directives about *tzitzit*, of the phrase: "I am the Lord your God who took you out of Egypt" (Numbers 15:41).

The *Or ha-Hayyim* (R. Hayyim ibn Attar; Morocco and the Land of Israel, 1696-1743) stated quite explicitly:

> *Tzitzit* testify that Israel are the servants of God.... Thus the Torah says, "You shall regard them and recall all of God's commandments" (Numbers 15:40), meaning that when they regard the symbol of their servitude they shall realize that they are not free to do whatever they please regarding food, dress, speech,

---

his garment to identify him as a slave," eerily reminiscent of the yellow patches/stars that were imposed upon Jews by medieval and modern oppressors.

and all their activities, just like a slave who is intimidated by his master.

And as the Rav summarized:

In leaving Egypt, the Jews exchanged a human master for a Divine Master, an oppressive, exploitative, and degrading service for a morally exalting and spiritually privileged service of the Lord. The Egyptian *kavla d'avda* was replaced by *tzitzit*.[60]

---

60. "The Symbolism of Blue and White," in Abraham R. Besdin (ed.): *Man of Faith in the Modern World: Reflections of the Rav Volume Two* (KTAV, 1989), 28.

THE NEXUS BETWEEN
REDEMPTION AND PRAYER

PREFACE
In this chapter, we shall discuss two additional dimensions of prayer—one hashkafic (philosophical) and one halakhic (juridical)—that we will consign under the rubric of "adjoining redemption to prayer" (*semikhat ge'ulah li-tefillah*).

TALMUDIC BACKGROUND
In the Talmud (*Berakhot* 4b), R. Yohanan declared: "Who merits the world to come? Whoever adjoins redemption to prayer in the evening service [*'arvit*]." The accompanying commentaries of Rashi and the Tosafot are enlightening.

RASHI
How much more so if he does it in the morning service [*shaharit*] because the essence of the

redemption from Egypt occurred during the morning, to wit: "On the morrow of the Pesah the Jews left [Egypt]" (Numbers 33:3). David, in Psalms, also alluded to adjoining redemption to prayer by saying: "God is my rock and my redeemer" (Psalms 19:15), soon followed by "God will answer you on a day of distress" (20:2). The Talmud Yerushalmi in *Berakhot* states: "To whom can we compare one who does not adjoin redemption unto prayer? To a courtier who knocks on the king's door and leaves before the king opens the door. Here, too, he has left."

Rather, one should bring God nigh to himself and appease Him with praise and encomium on account of the Exodus. God [then] will come nigh unto man, and as a result of that proximity, man can place his petitions before Him.

TOSAFOT (s.v. *de-amar Rabbi Yohanan*)
What about our own practice to recite other verses [between the blessing over redemption and the *'amidah* of *'arvit*][61]? It would appear

61. Referring, essentially, to *hashkiveinu* and *barukh Hashem le'olam.*

that since they are of rabbinic enactment [to allow latecomers to catch up so all the congregants could return home together] they constitute an "extended redemption" [rather than an interruption]. In addition, those verses contain eighteen references [to God] complementing the eighteen blessings of the 'amidah—apropos of which they also enacted the closing [prayer].

The *halakhah* follows R. Yohanan, whose position is supported by a *baraita*, and the *Halakhot Gedolot* also ruled in his favor. Therefore, it is prohibited to talk between the redemption [blessing] of 'arvit and the 'amidah. The Siddur of R. Amram Gaon, however, disagrees and stipulates that the recitation of Kaddish between redemption and prayer of 'arvit signifies that we do not require them to be brought nigh at that time, because the 'arvit service is optional.

This is problematic. R. Yohanan's position here indicates that he regards 'arvit as mandatory, and in a disagreement between R. Yohanan and Rav [who rules it is optional] we would be bound to follow R. Yohanan, so it is best to adopt a stringent position and beware of talking in between.

Alternatively, if there is a contradiction in *halakhah* we generally rule that *'arvit* is optional while here we appear to follow R. Yohanan who maintains it is mandatory—we would have to say that even if R. Yohanan agreed with Rav that *'arvit* is optional, he would still require that [redemption and prayer] be brought nigh, in which case we would do well to do so, too [and not interrupt].

THE HASHKAFIC DIMENSION:[62]
REDEMPTION IS THE GOAL OF THE
COVENANT, AND *SHEMA'* IS ITS EPITOME

The Rav began by defining his terms in such a way that *ge'ulah* and *tefillah* would share a common denominator. His definition of *ge'ulah* is the transition from silence to articulation, and his proof text is the Zoharic passage we cited earlier that states that Moses gave the Jewish people a voice (*ki ata Moshe, ata kol*).[63] To review: What is the connection between the episodes in which Moses protected a Jewish slave, interceding to stop a quarrel (2:11ff.), and the following statement: "And it came to pass in the course of many days… that the Children of Israel sighed on account of their bondage and they cried" (v. 23)? The *Zohar*'s explanation, expanded by the

62. Cf. "Lonely Man," 41, note.
63. See "Slavery and Redemption," above.

Rav, is that in the state of slavery the Jews were mute, incapable of sound, let alone articulate speech. They knew pain—in the physical sense—but not suffering; they thought their condition was normative. Only after Moses demonstrated to them that they were the victims of injustice did their sensitivity return, and, with it, their ability to cry out.

The ability to cry out to God is the prelude to prayer but not yet prayer itself. Crying out reflects an awareness of need, as the need of the sufferer for relief, but it does not yet recognize what the Rav calls "a hierarchy of needs." To cry out to God is to release pent up emotions almost arbitrarily; to pray to God is to have reflected on a variety of needs and to prioritize one's requests intelligently.

On the ladder of *ge'ulah*, *tefillah*, as the ability to articulate one's needs, is one rung above outcry. The highest rung, however, is Torah study (*talmud Torah*), which represents man's use of his intellectual abilities to discover his creative capacities. "When *tefillah* and *talmud torah* unite in one redemptive experience, prayer becomes *avodah shebalev*," which the Rav defined as an "offering of the heart" rather than the customary "service of the heart."[64] In this final stage of redemption, man prepares to return to God everything he is and could become, if so requested.

---

64. "Redemption," 70.

The proximity of prayer to redemption transforms it from merely a manner of expressing oneself in words into a veritable transcendent activity: a commitment to God and an acceptance of His moral authority. Redemption is the goal of the covenant, and *Shema'* is its epitome. Man has no right to come before God in quest of redemption without owning up to his covenantal commitments. As the Rav wrote: "Through prayer, they [Abraham, Isaac, Jacob, Moses, David and Solomon] achieved the covenant with God, and through prayer, we expect eventually to realize that covenant."[65] To promote this realization, *halakhah* imposed the requirement that redemption and prayer be seamless.

However, the intention required of the recitation of *Shema'* is not identical to that which is required of the *'amidah*. Whereas *Shema'* confers upon man the "ontological [existential] legitimacy" of a moral being engaged in a moral task, the *'amidah* forces man to appear before God as a humble, even enslaved, supplicant, ostensibly negating the very value of human existence. The condition that the Talmud (*Berakhot* 14b-15a) designates "accepting the yoke of heavenly majesty" (*kabbalat 'ol malkhut shamayim*) combines these two contradictory elements "into one comprehensive awareness of man who is at the same time the free messenger of God and his captive as well."[66]

---

65. "Redemption," 55.
66. "Lonely Man," 72.

THE HALAKHIC DIMENSION
We will enter the halakhic dimension via a didactic
dichotomy based upon the question introduced
by Tosafot (above): If bringing nigh redemption
unto prayer in *shaharit* precludes any interruption
between them, how does *'arvit* accommodate two—
and possibly even three[67]—interruptions?

Tosafot resolved the question by recourse to the
concept of "an extended [blessing of] redemption";
we shall deal with it by identifying the blessing
of redemption—in both *shaharit* and *'arvit*—as a
prerequisite (*mattir*) for the recitation of the *'amidah*,
paralleling the point made in the hashkafic dimension
just above. According to the Rav:

> ... *Tefillah* differs from all other *mitzvot* in
> which a person is obligated. With respect
> to other *mitzvot*, first the obligation of its
> performance falls upon the person. That
> obligation then transforms his [subsequent]
> action into the performance of a mitzvah, and
> awards it a special status.
>
> For example, a person assumes an
> obligation [to recite] a blessing following his
> nourishment and this obligation begets the

67. Depending on whether one's custom is to recite *barukh
Hashem le'olam*, or go directly from *hashkiveinu* to *hatzi
kaddish*.

[mitzvah] object of the grace after meals. So it is with regard to praise and thanksgiving; personal obligation is made manifest in the [subsequent] articulation of a blessing....

Tefillah, however, being a feature of [seeking divine] compassion and not a permanent fixture [i.e., the regular performance of a mitzvah], reverses the sequence. The blessings of prayer do not achieve the status of blessing—with all its signification and prerequisites—by means of an individual's obligation but on their own accord. There exists an object of *tefillah* in its fixed liturgy that is totally independent of personal obligation; [an object] whose prerequisite derives from its independent status as [seeking divine] compassion. Even if a person has already fulfilled his obligation [towards formal prayer], the signification of prayer as [seeking divine] compassion has not been removed... the obligation derives from the fact that it exists as an object of prayer in reality.[68]

Because the Rav saw *tefillah* as a perpetual constant rather than a discrete time-bound action, he maintained that women share with men the personal

68. Joseph B. Soloveitchik: *Shi'urim*, 40.

obligation to pray, despite the general perception that prayer belongs to a category of *mitzvot* from which women are exempt.

PRAYER AS DIALOGUE

TALKING WITH GOD

PREFACE

In "The Lonely Man of Faith," the Rav stipulated that "Adam II" requires a community to promote his redemption. The relationship between man and God in this community, which the Rav labeled "covenantal," is characterized by their proximity and even camaraderie. As he wrote:

> We meet God in the covenantal community as a comrade and fellow member. Of course, even within the framework of this community, God appears as the leader, teacher, and shepherd. Yet the leader is an integral part of the community, the teacher is inseparable from his pupils, and the shepherd

never leaves his flock…. The covenant draws
God into the society of men of faith.[69]

In this chapter, we shall see that the historical dialogue
between God and Moses, as well as the ongoing
dialogue between God and ourselves, epitomizes a
form of what I have termed "complementarity" that
constitutes an indispensable principle of the prayer
relationship between Man and God.

MUTUALITY AND *KAVVANAH*
The concept that God and Man express a collegial—
or even mutual—relationship through prayer[70]
appears to be the basis for a talmudic prescription
for the proper direction to which prayer should be
addressed (*Berakhot* 30a):

היה עומד בחוץ לארץ - יכוין את ליבו כנגד ארץ
ישראל שנאמר:(מלכים א' ח') והתפללו אליך דרך
ארצם. היה עומד בארץ ישראל - יכוין את לבו כנגד
ירושלים, שנאמר: (מלכים א' ח') והתפללו אל ה'
דרך העיר אשר בחרת; היה עומד בירושלים - יכוין
את לבו כנגד בית המקדש, שנאמר: (דברי הימים ב'
ו') והתפללו אל הבית הזה; היה עומד בבית המקדש
- יכוין את לבו כנגד בית קדשי הקדשים, שנאמר:
(מלכים א' ח') והתפללו אל המקום הזה;

69. "Lonely Man," 30.
70. See above: "Adam and the Rain."

היה עומד בבית קדשי הקדשים - יכוין את לבו כנגד
בית הכפורת; היה עומד אחורי בית הכפורת- יראה
עצמו כאילו לפני הכפורת; נמצא: עומד במזרח - מחזיר
פניו למערב, במערב - מחזיר פניו למזרח, בדרום-
מחזיר פניו לצפון, בצפון - מחזיר פניו לדרום; נמצאו
כל ישראל מכוונין את לבם למקום אחד.

One standing in the Diaspora should direct
his heart towards the Land of Israel... in
the Land of Israel—towards Jerusalem...
in Jerusalem—towards the Temple... in the
Temple—towards the Holy of Holies... in the
Holy of Holies—towards the *kapporet*... One
standing behind the *kapporet* should pretend
he is before it. The result is that one standing
in the east—faces west; ...west—faces east;
...south—faces north; and ...north—faces
south. The result is that all Israel direct their
hearts towards one place.

The *kapporet* became the narrowest focus of the
prayers of all Israel. Because it was from the *kapporet*
that the voice of God emanated in addressing Moses,
it is to that selfsame *kapporet* that Israel addresses its
voice in prayer.

ונועדתי לך שם ודברתי אתך מעל הכפרת מבין שני
הכרבים אשר על ארן העדת את כל אשר אצוה אותך
אל בני ישראל.

I shall meet with you there, and I shall speak
with you from above the *kapporet*, from
between the two cherubs [*keruvim*], which
are atop the Ark of the Covenant... (Exodus
25:22).

ובבא משה אל אהל מועד לדבר אתו וישמע את הקול
מדבר אליו מעל הכפרת אשר על ארן העדת מבין שני
הכרבים וידבר אליו.

When Moses entered the tent of meeting
to speak with Him, he heard the voice
discoursing with him from above the *kapporet*
atop the Ark of the Covenant, from between
the two cherubs [*keruvim*]... (Numbers 7:89).

KOFER, KAPPORET, KAPPARAH, AND YOM HA-KIPPURIM

The verbal root *k-p-r* is a homonymous one in the
Bible. The aspect with which we will deal here is the
one signifying the noun "pitch" (*kofer*), and the verb
"to coat [with pitch]" as in *ve-khafarta 'otah mi-bayit
u-mi-hutz ba-kofer*, "and you shall coat it, inside
and out with pitch" (Gen. 6:14). By metaphorical

extension, this also designates "to cover over, pacify, or propitiate," as in 'akhparah panav, "I shall pacify/propitiate him" (Gen. 32:21), and whence the noun kofer la-nefesh, "ransom, price of life," is derived.

Coming closer to our purpose—both textually and contextually—is 'ulai 'akhapperah be'ad hatta'tkhem, "You have erred/sinned grievously... perhaps I can cover over your error/sin" (Exodus 32:30). Rashi on this verse, appreciating both the literal and metaphorical usage of k-p-r, commented: "I shall place a coating [kofer], or filling [kinnu'ah], at the site of the sin, to keep you disengaged from it." Kofer, in these terms, is the stuff with which we fill in the chinks that sin causes to develop in our spiritual armor.

When do we apply this kofer? It is on the "Day of Atonement," a word that has a decidedly delicious derivation from the Middle English "at one," meaning "agreed." Yom ha-Kippurim is—literally as well as homiletically—a "Day of At-one-ment," or, recasting Rashi's metaphor, a "Day of Bonding." By closing the apertures of the soul and sealing them against erosion due to the friction of error and sin, Man becomes one with God and that is his ultimate kapparah.

The kapporet in the Tabernacle was a slab of pure gold that reposed atop the Ark of the Covenant (Exodus 25:17 ff.), fitted to its outer dimensions. Its relationship to the usages of the verbal root k-p-r that we have already demonstrated is also illustrated by its translation, in older English versions (based upon the Septuagint and the Vulgate), as "mercy seat," deriving its name from the notion of propitiation. In order to secure atonement (*kapparah*) for the Jewish people on the Day of Atonement (*Yom ka-Kippurim*), Aaron is instructed to sprinkle the blood of the sin-offering "on and before the *kapporet*" (Lev. 16:15-16).

CONCLUSION

Just as Moses at Sinai stood in the cleft of the rock clutching the tablets of the Law, as God in a cloud first revealed His attributes of compassion and grace, so was Aaron instructed to seek atonement for the Jewish people by replicating the circumstances of this revelation. The *kapporet* replaced the "cleft of the rock" (*nikrat ha-tzur*, Exod. 33:22) in which Moses stood, and the "cloud of incense" (*'anan ha-ketoret*, Lev. 16:13) replicated the "thickness of the cloud" (*'av he'anan*, Exod. 19:9) from within which God spoke.

We, who have neither the cleft of the rock nor the "mercy seat," and who can produce neither genuine clouds nor those of incense, must rely upon invoking the thirteen attributes of grace and compassion, and the *Selihot*, the liturgical order of *Yom ha-Kippurim*, invoking God's juridical capacity to pardon and atone.

Finally, it was only after Adam sinned and was banished from Eden that he was assigned the task "to work the earth whence he was taken" (Gen. 3:23). Assumedly, this is the juncture at which he prayed. Additional significance, then, attaches to the fact that immediately thereafter God set up two *keruvim* "to guard the way to the tree of life" (Gen. 3:24). These are, arguably, the same two *keruvim* that crowned the *kapporet* from between whose outstretched wings God spoke, and towards which Man directed his prayers.

THE IMPORTANCE OF EMPATHY[71]

TO KNOW IS TO EMPATHIZE

A particular focus of this chapter is the verse: "God saw the Israelites [*va-yar*'] and God knew [*va-yeda*']" (Exodus 2:25). What did He see and what did He know? There is a broad range of commentary on this question:

(1) **Onkelos:** The enslavement of the Israelites was exposed before God, and He decided to extricate them.

(2) **Saadiah Gaon:** God observed the Israelites and had compassion on them.[72]

(3) **Rashi:** He paid attention to them and did not overlook them.

---

71. "Empathy," 150-159.
72. In his (Arabic) commentary on Psalms 1:6, Saadiah enumerated no fewer than twelve uses of the verb *y-d-*'. Curiously, "to show compassion," his translation here, is not one of them.

(4) **Ibn Ezra (Long Commentary):** He saw that the Egyptians were [oppressing them] openly, and He knew what was being done secretly.

(5) **Ibn Ezra (Short Commentary):** Philosophers have stated that there are two categories of knowledge: knowledge of things that exist and knowledge of things that will be.

(6) **Ramban:** Rashi's interpretation is true to the manifest meaning (*peshat*). Initially, God hid His countenance from them and left them vulnerable. Now, He heard their cry and noticed them; i.e., He no longer hid Himself from them. He knew of their affliction and what they required. The text reveals several causes of their redemption: "God heard their cry and recalled His covenant" (Exodus 2:24), "For I have known his affliction" (3:7), because they were not yet worthy of redemption—although the time had come—as Ezekiel prophesied (20:6-10). It was only on account of their anguished cry that He compassionately accepted their prayers.

Combining all these nuanced definitions, we may suggest that "to know" is a multifaceted enterprise, including awareness and comprehension, intimacy and commitment. In the metaphysical domain indicated by our verse, it signifies empathy. God was already "aware" (cognitively) of their predicament, and "committed" (affectively) to their redemption; with the latest chapter in their travail, however, He became one with their suffering (behavioral).[73]

The Psalmist's phrase *'immo anokhi be-tzarah*, "I am with him in his distress" (Ps. 91:15) became the byword in talmudic-midrashic literature for the notion that when the Israelites were exiled from their land, God went into exile with them. He, so to speak, does not merely feel a distress similar to ours (sympathy); he sees our suffering as His own (empathy).

WHAT ELSE CAN WE "KNOW"?

According to Maimonides, we have an obligation to "know" God. Indeed, the very first laws of the *Mishneh Torah*, the "Foundational Torah Laws," begin with the stipulation that "the most fundamental principle and the pillar of all knowledge is to know that there is a first cause" (*Hilkhot Yesodei ha-Torah* 1:1). What sort of knowledge does that obligation entail? Are we to "know" Him the way He "knows" us?

Philosophy's answer has generally been that one knows God through the ability to provide rational proofs of His existence. The Rav, however, was critical

73. Cognitive, affective, and behavioral are the three domains in which educational objectives are customarily articulated. See Benjamin Bloom: *Taxonomy of Educational Objectives: The Classification of Educational Goals* (NY, 1956), passim.

of such proofs because they lack the experiential dimension he believed is indispensable to the true religious experience. He asked:

> Does the loving bride in the embrace of her beloved ask for proof that he is alive and real? Must the prayerful soul clinging in passionate love and ecstasy to her Beloved demonstrate that He exists? ...
>
> Maimonides' term "to know" transcends the bounds of the abstract *logos* and passes over into the realm of the boundless intimate and impassioned experience where postulate and deduction, discursive knowledge and intuitive thinking, conception and perception, subject and object, are one.[74]

TO TEACH IS TO EMPATHIZE

The Rav also regarded empathy as a prerequisite for successful pedagogy. In "Teaching with Clarity and Empathy," the Rav distinguished between the role that Moses played after the sin of the golden calf (Exodus 32), and the one he later played after the sin of the "graves of craving" (*kivrot ha-ta'avah*; Numbers 11).

---

74. "Lonely Man," 32-33, note. The Rav also observed there that Maimonides began by describing God in experiential ("aboriginal") terms and only in the fifth of those *halakhot* did he introduce a philosophical ("Aristotelian") proof for His existence.

To the former, Moses reacted as a teacher, making forceful pronouncements and taking forthright and powerful action. This, the Rav explained, was a suitable response to an incident involving idolatry.

The latter incident, however, was characterized by paganism and hedonism, and the "intellectual" approach of argument and persuasion that Moses took towards the golden calf would have been ineffectual. To counter this threat, he had to become a nursing father (*'omein*; Numbers 11:12):

> Besides teaching, he would have to reach out emotionally to the people, nurture them through their national infancy, with patient, sympathetic understanding and empathy....
>
> Our age is demonstrably pagan.... It consists of uninhibited *peritzut* (indulgence). The teaching role may have been sufficient in the past to counter the allurements of other religions, philosophies, and the pseudo-ideologies which still abound nowadays.... We must have, in addition to teaching: *dedication*, personal commitment, for otherwise the burden is unbearable; *selflessness*, a readiness to subordinate personal career and egotistical ambitions; and *empathy*, an ability to teach with feeling, not only with clarity.[75]

75. "Empathy," 157-158. Italics are in the original.

Given the tendency (noted in our introduction) of the Rav's provisions for prayer to traverse the lines that usually demarcate the intellectual rigor of the Mitnagdim from the emotional fervor of the Hasidim, we may posit that he would accept empathy as a component of mindfulness (*kavvanah*), a prerequisite for proper prayer.[76]

---

76. Cf. "Engaging the Heart and Teaching the Mind," comprising the Rav's eulogy for the Talner Rebbe, in Besdin: *Reflections of the Rav*, 160-168.

SPIRITUALITY AND COGNITION

A PEDAGOGICAL CHALLENGE:[77]
HOW TO TRANSMIT JUDAISM

The man of faith is "insanely" committed
to and "madly" in love with God.
— The Rav[78]

PREFACE

As articulated by Rabbi Kalonymus Kalman Shapira
(Poland; 1889-1943), the main principle of Hasidic
teaching is:

[T]hat a person must not consider it sufficient
that he has firmly placed his intellect into the

---

77. Pedagogical challenges are faced not only by
professional educators but by anyone who attempts or
intends to influence the transmission of Jewish values
including parents, rabbis, tutors, youth leaders, and, for
that matter, even neighbors and fellow-congregants who,
willy-nilly, serve as role models of religious attitudes and
behavior.
78. "Lonely Man," 61-62.

service of God. A connection made with the intellect alone is not a lasting connection. A person can subject his whole intellect to spiritual searching and can come to know with complete clarity of mind that he must serve only God in his every single thought, word, or action. And yet his heart and his whole body may still be very far away from this reality.[79]

Additionally, as Abraham Joshua Heschel wrote:

Mankind will not perish from want of information, but only for want of appreciation.[80]

The Rav had a perspective on spirituality that seems to combine disparate elements in his background and upbringing: the strictly rational, intellectual approach of the Brisk tradition, which he inherited from his father and grandfather; a more Hasidic approach that he acquired from his childhood tutor, a Lubavitch Hasid; and even a smattering of enlightenment that he obtained from his mother who would expose him to Russian literature and poetry.

---

79. Kalonymus Shapira: *A Student's Obligation* (NJ, 1991), 17.
80. Abraham Joshua Heschel: *God in Search of Man* (NY, 1955), 46.

THE INTELLECTUAL
DIMENSIONS OF THE SPIRIT

It is precisely in the realm of the intellect that enumerating the goals of spirituality falters. Such taxonomical terms as knowledge, comprehension, application, analysis, synthesis and evaluation[81] are seemingly inimical to a concept that comes with no specific set of subject-matter baggage.

It is possible, indeed, that spirituality is only behavioral-attitudinal and has no cognitive dimension. So, it appears, is the opinion of Howard Gardner who, in discussing a possible "spiritual intelligence," defined it as "primarily emotional or affective in character... and hence, again, ruled as beyond the confines of a cognitive investigation."[82]

I propose, to the contrary, that there *is* a cognitive side to spirituality. Moreover, I would argue that it is precisely this cognitive aspect that will allow us to map a spiritual curriculum and locate its coordinates among the normative cognitive goals of Jewish and general studies disciplines. To facilitate this consideration, I shall cite several of the operative definitions I have encountered among those modern and contemporary writers who have addressed

81. Bloom: *Taxonomy*, passim.
82. Howard Gardner in Jeffrey Kane (ed.): *Education, Information, and Transformation* (NJ, 1999), 121.

the relationship between spirituality and halakhic observance: Aryeh Kaplan, Yeshayahu Leibowitz, Abraham Joshua Heschel and, of course, the Rav. To provide a practical, educational consequence to their distinctions, I shall relate their comments to the use of rationales for *mitzvot* (*taʿamei ha-mitzvot*) as a pedagogical foil for the study and stimulus of *halakhah*, and conclude with a definitive pedagogical statement on this subject by Moshe Ahrend.

Aryeh Kaplan (USA; 1934-1983)

The main benefit of the commandments is in the realm of the spiritual. Observance of the commandments is ultimately the means through which a person brings himself close to God. As such, they are like nourishment to the soul. They strengthen man's soul, and at the same time, fortify him spiritually.[83]

• **Implications/Applications**

Mitzvot can become spiritually fortifying only as automatic responses, not as considered responses. Discussions of *taʿamei ha-mitzvot*, then, should

---

83. Aryeh Kaplan: *The Aryeh Kaplan Reader* (NY, 1983), 203.

either be curtailed or, at least, postponed until their performance is ingrained to the point of habit.[84]

Once this level of spiritual fortification is reached, discussion of the rationales of *mitzvot* becomes appropriate (Kaplan: "a great many mundane benefits") for the purpose of either reinforcement or as a *kiruv* tool to broach *mitzvot* to those who are not on a comparable spiritual level.

Yeshayahu Leibowitz

(Latvia, Germany, Israel; 1903-1994)

The first mark of the religion of Halakhah is its realism. It perceives man as he is in reality and confronts him with this reality—with the actual conditions of his existence rather than the "vision" of another existence…. It precludes the possibility of man shirking his duties by entertaining illusions of attaining a higher level of being…. Halakhic religion has no flair for the episodic excursions from the routine of everyday life, for the evanescent moments of solemnity… the *mitzvot* require observance out of a sense of duty and

---

84. Cf. Moshe Sokolow: "Knowledge and Action, Reason and Habit, in Jewish and Muslim Philosophies of Education," *Journal of Research on Christian Education* 22 (2013), 21-29.

discipline, not ecstatic enthusiasm or fervor, which may embellish one's life but do not tell how to conduct it. [85]

• **Implications/Applications**

While Kaplan saw *mitzvot* in the service of spirituality, Leibowitz saw them as divine dictates whose main—if not exclusive—purpose lies in their performance. Although they disagree on whether *mitzvot* are situated above or below the spiritual horizon (Leibowitz: "The fundamental and endearing elements of human existence are in life's prose, not in its poetry"), Leibowitz would agree to the postponement or elimination of discussions on *ta'amei ha-mitzvot* because faith is a value decision and cannot necessarily be reached as a logical deduction.

Abraham Joshua Heschel (Poland, USA; 1907-1972)

It is not only important what a person does; it is *equally* and even more important what a person *is*. Spiritually speaking, what he does is a minimum of what he is. Deeds are outpourings, they are not the essence of the self. Deeds reflect or refine but they remain

---

85. Yeshayahu Leibowitz: *Judaism, Human Values and the Jewish State* (Cambridge, 1992), 12-13.

functions. They are not the substance of
the inner life. Hence it is the inner life that
is the problem for us, Jewish educators, and
particularly the inner life of the Jewish child.
On the other hand, we must never forget
that in Judaism we answer God's will in
deeds. God asks for the heart, but the heart
is often a lonely voice in the market place of
living, oppressed with uncertainty in its own
twilight. God asks for faith and the heart is
not sure of its faith. It is good, therefore, that
there is a dawn of decision for the night of the
heart, deeds to objectify faith, definite forms
to verify belief.[86]

- **Implications/Applications**

Just as a book cannot be told from its cover, a person's
spirituality cannot be judged entirely by his or her
performance of *mitzvot*. On the other hand, a claim
to spirituality must rest on a minimum standard of
observance. In Heschel's scheme, *ta'amei ha-mitzvot*
have *a priori* status since they serve as a fulcrum
for the translation of spiritual desire into objective
religious reality.

---

86. Abraham Joshua Heschel: *The Insecurity of Freedom*
(Philadelphia, 1966), 232. Emphases in the original.

Joseph B. Soloveitchik

Most of all I learned [from my mother] that Judaism expresses itself not only in formal compliance with the law but also in a living experience. She taught me that there is a flavor, a scent, and warmth to *mitzvot*. I learned from her the most important thing in life—to feel the presence of the Almighty and the gentle pressure of His hand resting on my frail shoulders. Without her teachings, which quite often were transmitted to me in silence, I would have grown up a soulless being, dry and insensitive.[87]

- **Implications/Applications**

Ta'amei ha-mitzvot, for the Rav, seek to apprise us and to repeatedly remind us that behind every commandment is a benevolent commander whose instructions are intended to draw us nearer to Him and cement our relationship. A key pedagogical conclusion to draw from the Rav's reminiscence about his mother is the importance of role models in a person's life (see further below).

---

87. Joseph B. Soloveitchik: "A Tribute to the Rebbetzin of Talne," *Tradition* 17:2, 1978, 76-77.

Moshe Ahrend (France, Israel; 1926-2008)

Above all else it is vital that we project the *mitzvot* of the Torah as *mitzvot* of God and emphasize their legal and heteronomic character. They are neither rituals nor customs nor traditions; they are laws that the Supreme Legislator has imposed upon us, commanded us to observe, and by which He has sanctified us. Our obligation towards them does not depend either upon our consent or our comprehension, and we are commanded to fulfil them, not to analyze or internalize them. Moreover, even when we "comprehend" a mitzvah, its intentions and reasons, or we believe we comprehend it, this comprehension has no "legal" status and we are forbidden to draw halakhic conclusions from what appears to us to be the source or objective of a mitzvah....

Mitzvot are a symmetrical mesh of transcendent instructions that come to weave a tapestry of sanctity (*kedushah*), which has the capacity to elevate man precisely at the time when he is caught in the maelstrom of profane life and subjected to desires and passions that threaten to cause him to deteriorate and be demolished.[88]

---

88. Moshe Ahrend: "*Ta'amei haMitzvot*: Their Essence and their Place in Religious Education" (Hebrew), *Itturim* (Jerusalem, 1986), 81-83 (my translation). Reprinted in

- **Implications/Applications**

In advocating restraint in the use of *ta'amei ha-mitzvot*, Ahrend cautioned us not to exaggerate the importance of reason as though there actually were a sufficient answer to each and every question our students might pose. If everything were susceptible to rational analysis, he asked, what would be the purview of faith? His advice: Make *mitzvot* "reasonable" by means of Midrash and Aggadah, which conform to a person's levels of understanding, rather than through philosophy, which often just increases perplexity.

SPIRITUAL ROLE MODELS

Role-modeling for spirituality imposes certain prerequisites on both personality and pedagogy. Heschel advocated the following:

> What we need more than anything else is not *textbooks* but *textpeople*. It is the personality of the teacher which is the text that the pupils read; the text that they will never forget. The modern teacher, while not wearing a snowy beard, is a link in the chain of a tradition. He is the intermediary between the past and the present as well. Yet he is also the creator of the future of our people. He must teach the

Ahrend: *Hinnukh Yehudi be-Hevrah Petuhah* (Ramat Gan, 1995).

pupils to evaluate the past in order to clarify their future.[89]

The Rav, describing one of the dominant spiritual influences in his life—his tutor (*melammed*)—put it this way:

> However, besides teaching the *yeled zekunim* [youngster] discipline, the *av zaken* [father figure] teaches him something else—the romance of *Yahadut* [Judaism]. He teaches the child how to experience and feel *Yahadut*. *Yahadut* is not only discipline. Yes, we start with that, to discipline the child on all levels, on the physical level, on the social level, on the emotional level, and on the intellectual level. Above all, he teaches the child how to experience *Yahadut*, how to feel *Yahadut*. That is what my *melammed* taught me.[90]

Neither has the point been lost on contemporary educators:

> Soulful education, because it does not remain within the confines of logical empirical

---

89. Heschel: *The Insecurity of Freedom*, 237. Emphases in the original.
90. Joseph B. Soloveitchik: "The Future of Jewish Education in America," May 28, 1975. Cited by Aaron Rakeffet: *The Rav* (New Jersey, 1999), II, 178.

science, depends on living people. Its lessons cannot be found in books, computer programs, or floppy disks; they are not reducible to information that in some way can be processed.[91]

SPIRITUALITY IS A ROMANCE

The Rav also understood the value of experiential learning, describing it as the transmission of cultural experience from the preceding generation to the succeeding one:

A Jew is not only supposed to know what *Yahadut* stands for and to have knowledge of *Yahadut*; he is also called upon to experience *Yahadut*, to live it, and somehow to engage in a romance with the Almighty. Knowing about *Yahadut* is not enough; it is a norm to be implemented and experienced. It is to be lived and enjoyed. It is a great drama which the *yeled zekunim* must act out after observing the *av zaken*.

Studying the *Torah she-ba'al peh*, the Oral Tradition, and complying with its precepts are the greatest pleasures a person can have. It is an exciting and romantic adventure. It is the most cleansing and purging experience a

91. Jeffrey Kane: *Education*, 208.

human being can experience. The *av zaken* teaches the *yeled zekunim* how to live and feel *Yahadut.*[92]

ROMANCE PUT INTO PRACTICE

Rav Aharon Lichtenstein, in an address to the Educators Council of America, told the following story that transpired shortly after his Aliyah. He observed several Hareidi youngsters discussing whether, according to the Talmud in *Pesahim*, a secular Jew whose car was stuck was entitled to their help.

> I wrote a letter to the Rav at that time and I told him of the incident. I ended with the comment: Children of that age in our camp would not have known the *Gemara*. But they would have helped him. The feeling which I had then was: Why, *Ribbono shel Olam* [Master of the Universe] must this be our choice? Can't we find children who are going to help him and know the *Gemara*? Do we have to choose? I hope not; I believe not. If forced to choose, however, I would have no doubts where my loyalties lie; I prefer that they know less *Gemara*, but help him.[93]

92. Soloveitchik: "Future," 177-8.
93. Aharon Lichtenstein: "Developing a Torah Personality,"

SPIRITUALITY IN A
COMMUNITY OF SERVICE

To teach spirituality successfully, children cannot be the only ones participating. If we do not promote a collective spiritual ethic, we will be spinning our spiritual wheels in a futile exercise. Our institutions need to become the focal point of spiritual communities in which our children are exposed to a variety of role-models: teachers reinforce the formal lessons delivered in the classrooms during after-school activities; rabbis validate them in the synagogue; neighbors, in the market and the workplace; and parents, at home. Without this support system, we will be creating Jews whose experience with spirituality—like their experiences with a goodly portion of our formal curricula—is limited to the four cubits (*dalet amot*) of the study hall (*beit midrash*) and is not readily transferable to "real life."

In this respect, it is somewhat akin to prayer. Sadly, no matter how many times we teach the relevant laws in the *Mishnah Berurah*, how frequently, or successfully, we emphasize the prohibitions against conversation during prayer, or how much time we allocate to meditation before and concentration during prayer, one visit to a run-of-the-mill Shabbat

lecture #24; Yeshivat Har Etzion Israel Koschitzky Virtual Beit Midrash (http://www.etzion.org.il/).

service in a run-of-the-mill synagogue may undo
whatever spiritual good may have been accomplished
elsewhere.

Finally, the challenge of materialism demands
redress. As the Rav, with great foresight, already
noted in a 1968 address to the Rabbinical Council of
America:

> The problem with the American Jew is that
> he is not sensitive to Torah values. He must
> understand that human happiness does not
> depend upon comfort. The American Jew
> follows a philosophy which equates religion
> with making Jewish life more comfortable
> and convenient. It enables the Jew to have
> more pleasure in life. This de-emphasizes
> Judaism's spiritual values.[94]

And in a final nod to the importance of modeling, he
concluded:

> What the rabbi should do is somehow
> expose the Jew to proper Torah Judaism. This
> cannot be accomplished by preaching and
> sermonizing [alone]. Many times, as I know

---

94. Rakeffet: *The Rav*, vol. II, 18.

from my own experience, they accomplish
precisely the opposite.[95] [96]

---

95. Rakeffet, *The Rav*, vol. II, 18.
96. Adapted from Cf. Moshe Sokolow: "Teaching
Spirituality in Day Schools and Yeshiva High Schools," in
Adam Mintz and Lawrence Schiffman (eds.): *Spirituality
and Divine Law* (NY, 2004), 235-268.
Personally, I have a rather idiosyncratic view on
spirituality, as I do on similar terminologies that present
themselves as authentically Jewish, albeit in a vernacular
pose. I believe that any concept for which there is no
authentic biblical or rabbinic Hebrew equivalent is, *ipso
facto*, not an original Jewish concept. The common Hebrew
word for spirituality: *ruhaniyut*, came into existence only
in the twelfth century as an artificial word created by
Ibn Tibbon to translate the equivalent Arabic term. In
Muslim philosophical terminology, the term *rihaniya*—
utilized freely by the Geonim and by Maimonides—is the
antonym of the word for corporeality, *jismaniya*, for which
Ibn Tibbon also created the Hebrew word *gashmiyut*. If
you have ever wondered about the connection between
corporeality and rain (*geshem*), you now understand that
there is none. *Jism* is simply Arabic for a body.
An unfortunate and detrimental symptom of the
ubiquity of translations—even if unintentional—is the
now ingrained belief that English words we customarily
use in religious discourse (such as "nature," "miracles,"
"mercy," "repentance," and many others) have the exact
same values as more traditional Hebrew/Aramaic words.
See Moshe Sokolow: "*Rahamim* Does not Mean Mercy:
Etymological Scrupulousness and Torah Study" (Hebrew),
in Yotam Benziman (ed.): *Leshon Rabim; Ivrit ki-Sefat
Tarbut* (Jerusalem: Van Leer Institute, 2013), 194-200.

THE SINGULARITY OF
THE LAND OF ISRAEL

INSIGHTS INTO A
SEGULAH RELATIONSHIP[97]

PREFACE

We noted in the introduction that the Rav was an outspoken advocate of religious Zionism, who articulated a clarion call to modern Orthodox American Jews to support the nascent State of Israel and to tie their spiritual fortune to hers.[98] In this section, we will take a look at one of the underlying ideological foundations of the Rav's commitment to Israel: his insistence that *Eretz Yisrael*, *Am Yisrael*, and *Torat Yisrael* (the land of Israel, the nation of

---

97. Based on "The Singularity of the Land of Israel," in Abraham R. Besdin (ed.): *Reflections of the Rav* (Jerusalem, 1979), 117-126 (henceforth: "Singularity").
98. See below: "Fate, Destiny, and Shivat Tziyon"

Israel, and the Torah of Israel) embody singular relationships. These three principles are the pillars of the religious Zionist Mizrachi movement, which he served for many years as honorary president.

"The Singularity of the Land of Israel" explores the awesome power of opting to create bonds of deepest divine love between God, man, and the Land. According to the Rav, this active choice to experience divine love leads each Jew, as well as the entire Jewish people, into an intimate relationship with the Living God and with His "presence" within the Land of Israel.

DEFINING *SEGULAH*

The Rav explained that the word "singularity" (*segulah* in Hebrew) connotes "being only one," "exceptional," "extraordinary" and "separate."[99] In Exodus 19:5, the Torah enunciates the doctrine of the election of Israel as a cardinal tenet of our faith: "And you shall be to Me *segulah* from all other peoples." The word *segulah* is interpreted by Rashi as referring to "a cherished treasure, comparable to costly vessels and precious stones for which a king has a special regard."

---

99. The noun *segulah*, meaning "treasure," appears half a dozen times in the Bible, and a verb (*s-g-l*) appears in post-biblical Hebrew, meaning to acquire, save, or treasure. The Rav's essay is focused on its appearance in the phrase *'am segulah* (singular nation) in Exodus 19:5 (reiterated in Deut. 7:6; 14:2; and 26:18).

The people of Israel are a *segulah* people. Jews comprise a one of a kind nation that God has designated to preserve and disseminate His Torah. As Ovadiah Seforno (Italy; 1475-1550) commented on this verse:

> Although the entire human race is more valuable to me than any of the lower order creatures—because man alone is the intended [i.e., central] one, as the Rabbis said: "Man is beloved because he was created in a form" (Mishnah *Avot* 3:14)—in any event, you will be my most select of them all... and the distinction between you is quantitative: for the entire land is indeed mine, and the righteous among the nations of the world are undoubtedly dear to me as well.

SEGULAH BY ANALOGY TO MARRIAGE

A Mishnah stipulates:

> A man may betroth [a woman] in person or through an agent. A woman can accept betrothal directly or via an agent. A man may betroth his daughter, while she is [still] an adolescent, personally or via an agent (*Kiddushin* 41a).

And the Talmud (*Kiddushin* 41a) elaborates:

> If an agent can betroth, surely [the principal] can? [But] R. Yosef said: It is a greater mitzvah to do so personally than via an agent....
>
> Others say that [delegating betrothal to an agent] involves a prohibition, as R. Yehudah taught in the name of Rav: It is prohibited for a man to betroth a woman sight unseen lest he [subsequently] discover in her something offensive and reject her, and God has cautioned us to "love your neighbor as yourself" (Lev. 19:19).

The Rav illustrated this principle by way of the Torah's account of Isaac's marriage to Rebecca.

> Isaac brought [Rebecca] to his mother Sarah's tent; he took Rebecca to be his wife and he loved her; and Isaac was consoled after his mother's [death] (Gen. 24:67).

To which Rashi commented:

> He took her to the tent and she became his mother Sarah; i.e., she became a paradigm of Sarah. While Sarah lived, a candle burned on Fridays and the dough was blessed; when she died, they ceased, and were restored when Rebecca came.

In other words, although Abraham's servant had given assurance of Rebecca's sterling attributes, Isaac still allowed some time to elapse before marrying her—ostensibly, in order to acquaint himself personally with her character. As the Rav added:

> Such a commitment, if it is to be whole-hearted, without reservations, and for all time, can only be derived from first-hand knowledge. That explains the prohibition of marrying someone without prior acquaintance and affection.[100]

SEGULAH BY ANALOGY TO "SCOUTING"

Just as an impending marriage requires prior personal inspection, the mating of a nation and its homeland required a similar enterprise. Hence, Moses dispatched scouts[101] to report on the Land of Canaan.

There is a glaring contradiction between the account the scouts narrated, at length, in Numbers, and its abbreviated recap in Deuteronomy. In the first case, the initiative seemed to have been God's:

---

100. "Singularity," 122.
101. The Rav was insistent that they were not spies, per se, because most of the information they were instructed to obtain was not military in nature: "Our conclusion, therefore, is that we are dealing with explorers and scouts, not spies" (118).

> God spoke to Moses saying: Dispatch men to scout out the Land of Canaan that I am giving to Israel, one man per tribe… (Numbers 13:1 ff.).

While in the latter, it clearly belonged to the people:

> You all approached me and suggested that we send men to explore the land…. I approved the suggestion and chose twelve men… who spied it out (Deuteronomy 1:22-24).

The resolution appears to be that after the people approached Moses with their suggestion, he referred it to God, whose approval, couched in Numbers 13:2 as, literally, "Send men for *yourself*" (*shelah lekha 'anashim*), can be read as a cautionary note distancing *Himself* from the decision.[102] The consequences that ensued can therefore be imputed to Moses and Israel, rather than to God.

Among the questions raised by the Rav concerning the scouting mission is why the Israelites would require any intelligence about the Land of Canaan when the miraculous nature of the Exodus and the crossing of the sea surely had made such mundane steps unnecessary, at best, and reflecting downright distrust of God, at worst. Had they not been promised by that very Divine Authority that the

---

102. See Ramban, ad. loc.

land towards which they were heading was "flowing with milk and honey" (Exodus 3:8, 17)? The Rav concluded that the scouting mission must, therefore, have had a different purpose:

> This, we suggest, was the reason Moses was told to send scouts into the land— not to gather intelligence, but to have the distinguished heads of each tribe explore the land and bring back reports of its singular character. The instructions Moses gave them defined their mission, viz. to make the acquaintance of the land. By entering the land, the people were being wedded to it and, despite Divine assurances of its quality, they had to experience it through their princes before the commitment could be deeply rooted and irrevocably assumed.[103]

Like Isaac's betrothal to Rebecca, "A commitment granted through proxy information is inevitably limited and qualified."[104]

A *SEGULAH* RELATIONSHIP BETRAYED
As the Rav stated:

---

103. "Singularity," 122.
104. "Singularity."

A singular *segulah* people, special to God, was being joined to a singular land, from which God's attention is never withdrawn. [Cf. Dt. 11:12] Destinies were being joined.[105]

Although a cursory reading of the scouts' report might lead one to conclude that they had merely fulfilled their assigned tasks, a closer look at the text brings to light a number of troubling aspects of their accounting.[106] From the Rav's perspective, however, the greatest of their sins was committed against the singular relationship that the Jewish nation was intended to have with its land.

Contrary to Moses's expectations, not only did the scouts fail to acknowledge such a relationship, but their rejection of God's Promised Land was tantamount to a rejection of the covenant He had made with Abraham, in which He had stated: "To your descendants, I will give this land" (Gen. 15:18).

Their report was that of spies, not that of scouts; they balanced debits against credits and declared the entire enterprise hopeless. With grandeur looking down on them, all they could see was the mundane.[107]

---

105. "Singularity."
106. A detailed examination, utilizing numerous commentaries, is available in Nehama Leibowitz: "The Twelve Spies," in Idem: *Torah Insights* (Jerusalem, 1995), "The Twelve Spies" (1-19).
107. "Singularity," 123.

SEGULAH UNRECOGNIZED: ADJOINING MIRIAM

According to the Rav's understanding of the interconnectedness of the land, the nation, and the Torah, the rejection of one is the equivalent of the rejection of them all. In this manner, he addressed a question of narrative contiguity (*semikhut ha-parashiyot*) that concerned the major exegetes.

The Torah portion immediately preceding that of the scouts recounts the punishment suffered by Miriam on account of her taking the lead in protesting Moses's treatment of his wife.[108] There are those who stated that there was a reason for its placement right before the account of the scouts, while yet others maintained that this was merely coincidental. Rashi wrote:

Why does the portion of the scouts adjoin that of Miriam? Because she was punished for slandering her brother [Moses] and these evildoers witnessed this and missed the moral.

108. "Which wife?" is a question to which exegetes have given two distinct answers. The more traditional response is the only wife about whom we are explicitly informed, namely Zipporah. The problem is that she was Midianite, and Numbers 12:1 says the complaint against Moses was lodged on account of his Cushite wife. This prompted other exegetes to posit the existence of a second wife, a Cushite, about whom the Torah is otherwise silent. See, e.g., Yosef Ibn Kaspi, cited in Moshe Sokolow: *TANAKH: An Owner's Manual* (New York: Ktav/Urim, 2015), 128.

To the Rav, however, Miriam's crime was her denial of the singularity of Moses's prophetic status and that anticipated and approximated the scouts' disavowal of the singularity of the Land of Israel.

> The tragedy of Miriam and the scouts was their failure to note the uniqueness which surrounds the *segulah* dimension of all aspects of Jewish existence. This explains the inability of non-Jews to understand the depth of attachment which the Jew, to this very day, has to this land. They view this bond solely in secular, nationalistic terms. The intense, passionate involvement of Jews today throughout the world with the Land of Israel testifies to an identification which transcends normal devotion and, instead, reflects a fusion of identities, the *segulah* dimension…

The Rav's conclusion appeals to us to recognize when we are being summoned to a higher purpose.:

> A *segulah* prophet was leading a *segulah* people into a *segulah* land. The response of the scouts, however, was pedestrian. [109]

---

109. "Singularity," 123.

FATE, DESTINY, AND *SHIVAT TZIYYON*

THE RAV ON RELIGIOUS ZIONISM

PREFACE

On Yom ha-Atzma'ut 1956, the Rav delivered a public address at Yeshiva University entitled *Kol Dodi Dofek* ("Hark, My Beloved Knocks").[110] This address, which has become a classic of religious Zionist philosophy, enumerated and elaborated upon the instances of God's tangible presence in the recent history of the Jewish people and the State of Israel. It also issued a clarion call to American Orthodoxy to embrace the State of Israel and commit itself and its resources to its development.

---

110. We have chosen the translation that appears in Joseph B. Soloveitchik: *Fate and Destiny: From the Holocaust to the State of Israel* (NY: Ktav, 1992). A Hebrew version, בסוד היחיד והיחד (Orot, 1976) was published by Pinchas Peli.

We shall deal here with the latter portion of this 60-page address, specifically, with the distinction the Rav drew between two forms of covenant: "The Covenant of Fate" (*berit goral*), and "The Covenant of Destiny" (*berit yi'ud*). In developing these themes, the Rav treated—halakhically and homiletically—the narratives of the Exodus and the Revelation of the Law. In that process, he also outlined a position on conversion to Judaism that is particularly poignant in light of the ongoing controversy in Israel and abroad over this matter.

SIX KNOCKS[111]

First, the knock of the Beloved was heard in the political arena. No one can deny that from the standpoint of international relations, *the establishment of the State of Israel, in a political sense, was an almost supernatural occurrence.*[112]

---

111. The Rav's terminology derives from the Song of Songs (*Shir ha-Shirim*). Its protagonists are a beloved (*dod*), who, in a work traditionally regarded as allegorical, represents God, and his beloved (*ra'yah*), who represents the people of Israel. In his quest for her, the beloved knocks on her door six times but she fails to respond and open it for him.
112. "Fate and Destiny," 26 (italics in the original).

The Rav, acknowledging the "unholy" alliance of the West and the Soviet Union in the recognition of the Jewish state, ruminated over the possibility that the entire organization of the United Nations came into being solely in order to facilitate the establishment of Israel. And so, on Nov. 29, 1947, when the U.N. General Assembly voted to partition the British Mandate for Palestine into Jewish and Arab states and the chairman banged his gavel to call the role, the Rav heard the sound of the Beloved knocking.

Second, the knocking of the Beloved could be heard on the battlefield. *The small Israeli Defense Forces defeated the mighty armies of the Arab countries.* The miracle of "the many in the hands of the few" took place before our very eyes.[113]

On the analogy of the Exodus—where Pharaoh hardened his heart and suffered a worse deal than was originally offered him—the Rav considered the Arab attack a blessing in disguise. Had they accepted the partition plan as voted and not attacked, Israel would have had to settle for a state that excluded Jerusalem, a large part of the Galilee, and vast parts of the Negev.

---

113. "Fate and Destiny," 27.

Third, the Beloved began to knock as well on the door of the theological tent, and it may very well be that this was the strongest knock of all…. All the claims of Christian theologians that God deprived the Jewish people of its rights in the land of Israel, and that all the biblical promises regarding Zion and Jerusalem refer, in an allegorical sense, to Christianity and the Christian Church, *have been publicly refuted by the establishment of the State of Israel and have been exposed as falsehoods*, lacking all validity.[114]

Christianity had declared the Jewish covenant with God to be terminated—that is the real meaning of their term Old Testament (*ha-Berit ha-Yeshanah*)—and declared themselves the "new" Israel. The powerlessness of Jews throughout the Middle Ages and at the beginning of the modern period reinforced this impression. The Rav spoke of the particular pleasure he derived from references to "Israel" in Christian newspapers, and experienced a special delight upon reading in a United Press release on the eve of Passover that "the Jews will sit down tonight at the Seder table confident that the miracles of Egypt will recur today."

---

114. "Fate and Destiny," 27.

Fourth, the Beloved is knocking in the hearts of the perplexed and assimilated youths. The era of self-concealment (*hester panim*) at the beginning of the 1940s resulted in great confusion among the Jewish masses and, in particular, among the Jewish youth.... Buried, hidden thoughts and paradoxical reflections emerge from the depths of the souls of even the most avowed assimilationists. And once a Jew begins to think and contemplate, once his sleep is disturbed—who knows where his thoughts will take him, what form of expression his doubts and queries will assume?[115]

The ability, almost mystical, of even a brief visit to the State of Israel to restore to some degree the Jewish identities of even the most alienated Jewish young people is the stuff of which legends are made. The Rav posited that "it is good for a Jew not to be able to hide from his Jewishness." Comparing self–hating Jews to Jonah, he said that they would find no refuge in the innermost depths of their respective ships. Like Jonah, again, when asked, "Who are you?" they should answer, "I am a Hebrew, and I fear the Lord, the God of heaven" (Jonah 1:9).

---

115. "Fate and Destiny," 29-31.

The fifth knock of the Beloved is perhaps the most important of all. For the first time in the history of our exile, divine providence has surprised our enemies with the sensational discovery that Jewish blood is not free for the taking, is not *hefker*![116]

Unapologetically, the Rav argued for the moral right and responsibility of the Jewish nation to defend itself. Even though *halakhah* interprets "an eye for an eye" (Exod. 21:24) figuratively as monetary compensation, the Rav argued: "With regard to Nasser and the Mufti I would demand that we interpret the phrase… in a strictly literal sense as referring to the removal of the concrete, actual eye…. Revenge is forbidden when it serves no purpose. However, if by taking revenge we raise ourselves up to the plane of self-defense, then it becomes the elementary right of man *qua* man to avenge the wrongs inflicted upon him."[117] The readiness of the State of Israel to unleash its armies against its enemies is the surest and most effective deterrent to the renewal of the venomous type of anti-Semitism which declares open season on Jewish blood.

---

116. "Fate and Destiny," 29-31.
117. "Fate and Destiny," 32.

The sixth knock, which we must not ignore, was heard when the gates of the land were opened. A Jew who flees from a hostile country now knows that he can find a secure refuge in the land of his ancestors. Now that the era of divine self-concealment (*hester panim*) is over, Jews who have been uprooted from their homes can find lodging in the Holy Land.[118]

Subsequent events have, again, validated the Rav's insight. While he had in mind the mass migration of North African and Oriental Jews of the early 1950s, we can add the recent, and equally massive, Aliyah of Jews from the Former Soviet Union and Ethiopia. In this context, the Rav also speculated on what might have been had the State of Israel come into existence before the Holocaust.

THE COVENANT OF FATE: *BERIT GORAL*

When God issued His promise of redemption to the Jews in Egypt, He made a covenant with them, proclaiming: "I will take you for Me as a people and I will be for you as a God" (Exodus 6:7). When the Torah was given at Sinai, a second covenant was made: "And [Moses] took the account of the covenant... and said, 'Behold the blood of the covenant which the Lord has

---

118. "Fate and Destiny," 34.

cut with you by means of all these words'" (Exodus 24:7-8). (The second covenant was reiterated in the plains of Moab (Deuteronomy 28:69), leading the Talmud in *Berakhot* 48b to claim that the Torah was "given with three covenants.")

Question: How did the two covenants differ from one another?

Answer: The obvious answer is that the first covenant was made while the Jews were still enslaved in Egypt, whereas the second was made after their liberation.

Question: Can a slave enter into a covenant? What significance, or binding force, can a covenant have (it is, essentially, a mutually binding legal contract) when one of the parties is not able to act freely?

Answer: The inability to act freely is exactly (although paradoxically) what "fate" is all about. The lowly status of the slave and the existential experience of loneliness and helplessness with which it is synonymous, are precisely the prerequisites for a covenant of fate.

As the Rav noted:

> When the Jew, with this sense of his special, unique fate, confronts God face to face, he encounters the God of the Hebrews, who reveals himself to man from out of the very midst of the experience of loneliness and necessity, from out of the very midst of the consciousness of the fate which seizes hold of an individual and overcomes him.
>
> The God of the Hebrews does not wait for man to search for Him, to freely invite Him into his presence. He imposes His rule over man, against his will. A Jew cannot expel the God of the Hebrews from his private domain... he serves the God of the Hebrews against his will.[119]

Question: What are the consequences of this covenant of fate?

Answer: The Rav enumerates four positive consequences of the awareness of a shared fate:

1. *shared historical circumstances*
2. *shared suffering*
3. *shared responsibility and liability*
4. *shared activity*

---

119. "Fate and Destiny," 45.

Shared Historical Circumstances

The lowest common denominator of the covenant of fate is that, historically, Jews have been regarded and treated alike. Neither exile, nor persecution, nor attempts at genocide have bothered to discriminate amongst Jews on grounds of social status, economic privilege, or religious observance. In Mordechai's words to Esther: "Do not imagine that you, of all the Jewish people, can escape in the palace" (Esther 4:13). In the Rav's words: "*Haverim kol Yisrael*: All Israel are knit together—We will all be pursued unto death or we will all be redeemed with an eternal salvation."[120]

Shared Suffering

A logical, and natural, consequence of the awareness of a shared predicament would be a commonality of anguish: the sharing by Jews of each other's suffering. To illustrate this point, the Rav utilized a homily based upon the discussion of the legacy to which a man with two heads is entitled (Tosafot, *Menahot* 37a, s.v. *o kum*).

---

120. "Fate and Destiny," 47. This point is reiterated in the Rav's exposition of Amalek; see "A Time for Spiritual Sobriety," below.

Question: Does he receive two shares, or just one; does he constitute two separate entities inhabiting the same body, or just a single entity with diverse appearances?

Answer: The answer is to have boiling water poured on one of the heads. If it alone cries out in pain, then it is truly separate from the other; if both experience the agony, however, then there is but one.

As the Rav interpreted this:

If boiling water is poured upon the head of the Jew in Morocco, the fashionably attired Jew in Paris or London has to scream at the top of his voice, and through feeling the pain he will remain faithful to his people.[121]

Shared Responsibility and Liability

"All Jews are guarantors for one another" (*kol Yisrael 'areivim zeh ba-zeh*). This is not merely a lofty philosophical aspiration; it functions, in *halakhah*, as a principle of law.

---

121. "Fate and Destiny," 49.

Question: What is an example of the halakhic application of this principle?

Answer: The rule that anyone may assist another to fulfill a halakhic obligation even if he has already fulfilled it himself. If we were not inextricably linked to one another, we would not be concerned about one another—let alone manifest concern about one another's discharge of responsibility.

Question: What is the Torah source for this concept of 'arevut?

Answer: The Sages (*Sotah* 37b) derived it from Deuteronomy 29:28: "The hidden things belong to the Lord, our God; but the things that are revealed belong to us and to our children forever, to observe all the words of this Torah." As Rashi commented there: "When they crossed the Jordan and had the oath administered to them at Mt. Gerizim and Mt. Ebal, they became responsible for one another."

The Rav extrapolated yet further:

> The commandment of the sanctification of
> the divine Name and the prohibition against
> the desecration of the divine Name can
> be explained very well in the light of this
> principle of shared responsibility and liability.
> The actions of the individual are charged to
> the account of the community. Any sin he
> commits besmirches the name of Israel in the
> world. The individual, therefore, must answer
> not only to his own personal conscience but
> also to the collective conscience of the people.
> If he behaves properly, he sanctifies the name
> of Israel and the Name of the God of Israel;
> if he sins, he casts shame and disgrace on the
> people and desecrates the Name of its God.[122]

Shared Activity

While the consequences of shared fate we have
already cited appear negative, there is also a strikingly
positive aspect. First of all, we have a proverb that
states: "A shared predicament is a partial consolation"
(*tzarat rabbim hatzi nehamah*). The mutuality of
historical experience, the reciprocity of anguish, and
the bearing of a communal burden are not entirely
negative characteristics; they have obvious and

122. "Fate and Destiny," 52.

significant redeeming value that the Rav called "a unifying consciousness in the field of social action."[123] As he wrote in the concluding portion of this part of the essay:

We have stated that it is the consciousness of the fate imposed upon the people against their will and of their terrible isolation that is the source of the people's unity, of their togetherness. It is precisely this consciousness as the source of the people's togetherness that gives rise to the attribute of *hesed*, which summons and stirs the community of fate to achieve a positive mode of togetherness through ongoing, joint participation in its own historical circumstances, in its suffering, conscience, and acts of mutual aid.

The lonely Jew finds consolation in breaking down the existential barriers of egoism and alienation, joining himself to his fellow and actively connecting himself with the community. The oppressive sense of fate undergoes a positive transformation when individual personal existences blend together to form a new unit—a people. The obligation to love one another stems from the consciousness of this people of fate, this

123. "Fate and Destiny," 53.

lonely people that inquires into the meaning of its own uniqueness. It is this obligation of love that stands at the very heart of the covenant made in Egypt.[124]

THE COVENANT OF DESTINY: *BERIT YI'UD*

As opposed to the covenant of fate, which was made with a slave people who had no free will to exercise, the covenant of destiny was made with a free nation which could, and did, make up its own mind. God did not simply impose the Torah on Israel; He offered it to them—via Moses—and awaited their response of "we shall act and we shall listen" (*na'aseh ve-nishma'*).

Question: What is the difference between fate and destiny?

Answer: Fate is uncontrollable, destiny can be directed.

Destiny in the life of a people, as in the life of an individual, signifies a deliberate and conscious existence that is chosen out of free will and in which the realization of an historical mission is found.

Slaves merely exist; they anticipate no change in their reality. Free men, on the other hand, generally aspire to forward and upward movement in their lives. The Torah provides the Jewish nation with a road

---

124. "Fate and Destiny," 53-54.

map to its destiny; Jewish history is the benchmark of the extent to which that road has been properly traveled.

Question: Is this difference reflected in the Torah's forms of address?

Answer: Yes. There are two pairs of corresponding Hebrew terms which embody this distinction. The first is *'am*, as opposed to *goy*, and the second is *mahaneh*, as opposed to *'edah*.

As a people (*'am*, coming from the word *'im*, meaning "with"), the Hebrews had no way to determine their own fate; as a nation (*goy*, related to the word *geviyah*, "body"), however, they have the ability to forge their own destiny. At Sinai, God offered them the opportunity to become a holy nation (*goy kadosh*). Whether they would take up the challenge and execute it properly was their choice and would determine their destiny.

A *mahaneh* (camp) designates a coming together for protection and self-defense; it is a product of fate. An *'edah* ("congregation," from the same root as *'eid*, "witness"), on the other hand, is created as result of the recognition of a shared past, but also of mutual aspirations, i.e., a common destiny. As the Rav put it:

The Hebrew word for nation is *goy*, which is related to the word *geviyah*, body. The *'am hesed*, the people of loving kindness, was raised on high and became a *goy kadosh*, a holy nation. Holiness, which expresses itself in an authentic mode of being, is the very foundation of the shared destiny of a nation.[125]

The congregation is a holy nation that has no fear of fate and is not compelled to live against its will. It believes in its own destiny, and it dedicates itself, out of its own free will, to the realization of that destiny. The covenant in Egypt was made with a people born from a camp; the covenant at Sinai was made with a holy nation.[126]

CIRCUMCISION AND IMMERSION
The Conversion from Fate to Destiny

Question :   The actual departure from Egypt merely freed the Jews from slavery. What transformed them from a people into a nation and gave them control over their destiny?

---

125. "Fate and Destiny," 56.
126. "Fate and Destiny," 60.

Answer: According to Hazal, they underwent *giyyur*, a process of conversion, which included both of the ritual prerequisites for contemporary conversion: circumcision (*milah*) and immersion (*tevilah*).

A disagreement existed amongst the Geonim and Rishonim as to whether both circumcision and immersion were required for everyone before both the Exodus and revelation of the Law. The alternatives, which the Rav discussed in depth in a lengthy footnote,[127] relate to the different status of men vs. women and of Levites vs. the remainder of the Israelites. The Rav, as usual, took the side of Maimonides, whose opinion in this matter he summed up as follows:

> Israel entered into the covenant by way of three rites: circumcision, immersion, and sacrifice. Circumcision took place in Egypt... Immersion took place in the wilderness before the revelation of the Torah... [as were the sacrifices] (*Hilkhot Issurei Bi'ah* 13:1-3).

A disagreement similarly exists regarding the question of which procedure, circumcision or immersion, took precedence over the other, whether

127. "Fate and Destiny," note 23, p. 82ff.

that is an absolute precedence, and what relationship these processes bear to the overall requirement of accepting the yoke of the commandments (*kabbalat 'ol mitzvot*). The Rav again cited chapter and verse in Maimonides:

> A convert who was not examined or who was not informed about the commandments and the punishments [for transgressing them], but was circumcised and immersed in the presence of three laymen [i.e., as opposed to a formal *beit din*], is deemed a [valid] convert (*Hilkhot Issurei Bi'ah* 13:7).

Question: Does this imply that a convert does not have to accept the *mitzvot*? Does this imply that the Chief Rabbinate of Israel and its supporters have been holding out for what amounts to a stringency (*humra*) in the law and not something essential?

Answer: Absolutely not! The Rav continued to explain:

I once heard from my father and master [R. Moshe Soloveitchik], of blessed memory, that Maimonides does not mean to say that a person who converted with the intention of not observing the commandments is deemed a valid convert. Such a notion would subvert the entire concept of conversion and the holiness of Israel, which exhausts itself in our obligation to fulfill God's commandments.

Maimonides' position is that the acceptance of the commandments, unlike immersion, does not constitute a distinct act in the process of conversion that would require the presence of a court. Rather, acceptance of the commandments is a defining feature of the conversion process that must be undergone for the sake of fulfilling the commandments.

Therefore, if we know that the convert, at the time of immersion, is willing to accept the yoke of the commandments, the immersion effects conversion even though there was no special act of informing the convert about the commandments and his consenting to fulfill them, since the convert intends to live the holy life of an observant Jew.

It would appear, however, that the view of the Tosafot, cited earlier, is that the acceptance of the commandments is a distinct element in the conversion process and, consequently, that the law necessitating the presence of a court refers to the court's presence at the act

of acceptance. Only this act of acceptance—
and not immersion—requires the presence of
the court.[128]

THE OBLIGATION OF TORAH
JEWRY TO THE LAND OF ISRAEL

Question: Have the expectations of Zionism
been met with the creation of a
Jewish state?

Answer: Not entirely. The Rav observed
that the political and geographical
integrity of the State of Israel would
be enhanced immeasurably by the
increased colonization of the Land
of Israel. He feared that allowing
the land to remain desolate was
tantamount to relinquishing
sovereignty over it, and argued that
the conquest of the Negev had to be
followed by its settlement.

Question: What of the particular goals of
religious Zionism?

---

128. "Fate and Destiny," note 24, p. 91ff.

Answer: Statehood, per se, was never the goal of religious Zionism, which yearned for a return to the Torah of Israel along with the return to the Land of Israel. It is not even enough for religious Zionists just to settle in Israel. They must use their presence in the country to inspire its citizens and their leaders to increase their devotion to Torah.

Question: To what does the Rav attribute the antagonism between religious and secular Zionism?

Answer: According to the Rav, secular Zionism erred in espousing and advocating "normalcy," the doctrine (often called the *niheyeh ke-khol ha-goyim* syndrome) that projects the goal of Zionism as creating a country similar to other nation-states. While intended, in part, to reduce those dangers of anti-Semitism that emanate from hostility towards "others" and to reduce the Jewish feeling of isolation from the world, it stands in sharp contradiction to both the concepts of fate (*goral*) and destiny (*yi'ud*).

He wrote:

> If you were to ask me: What is the task of the
> State of Israel? I would answer: The mission
> of the State of Israel is neither the termination
> of the unique isolation of the Jewish people
> nor the abrogation of its unique fate—in
> this it will not succeed!—but the elevation
> of a camp-people to the rank of a holy
> congregation-nation and the transformation
> of shared fate to shared destiny.[129]

Question: In the Rav's estimation, has Religious Zionism met this challenge?

Answer: No. As he wrote:

> Let us be honest and speak openly and
> candidly. We are critical of certain well-
> known Israeli leaders because of their
> attitudes to traditional values and religious
> observances. Our complaints are valid; we
> have serious accusations to level against the
> secular leaders of the land of Israel. However,
> are they alone guilty, while we are as clean
> and pure as the ministering angels? Such an
> assumption is completely groundless!

---

129. "Fate and Destiny," 70.

We could have extended our influence in shaping the spiritual image of the Yishuv if we had hastened to arouse ourselves from our sleep and descend to open the door for the Beloved who was knocking. I am afraid that we Orthodox Jews are, even today, still sunk in a very pleasant slumber. Had we established more religious kibbutzim, had we built more houses for religious immigrants, had we created an elaborate and extended system of schools, our situation would be entirely other than it is. Then we would not have to criticize the leaders of other movements so severely.[130]

Question: Did the Rav have a prescription for remedying the situation?

Answer: Yes; he prescribed graciousness (*hesed*) inspired and directed by Torah ethics and values. As he wrote in the concluding paragraph of the entire essay:

Our historic obligation, today, is to raise ourselves from a people to a holy nation, from the covenant of Egypt to the covenant at Sinai, from an existence of necessity to an authentic way of life suffused with eternal

---

130. "Fate and Destiny," 38 ff.

ethical and religious values, from a camp to a congregation.

The task confronting the religious *shivat ziyyon* movement is to achieve that great union of the two covenants—Egypt and Sinai, fate and destiny, isolation and solitude. This task embraces utilizing our afflictions to improve ourselves, and it involves spinning a web of *hesed* that will bind together all the parts of the people and blend them into one congregation, "one nation in the land"; it involves the readiness to pray for one's fellow, and empathy with his joy and grief....

One great goal unites us all, one exalted vision sets all our hearts aflame. One Torah— the Written Torah and the Oral Torah— directs all of us toward one unified end: the realization of the vision of solitude, the vision of a camp-people that has ascended to the rank of a holy congregation-nation, bound together its fate with its destiny, and proclaims to the entire world, in the words of our ancient father, Abraham: "And I and the lad will go yonder, and we will worship and we will return to you" (Genesis 22:5).[131]

---

131. "Fate and Destiny," 74.

A TIME FOR SPIRITUAL SOBRIETY: THE RAV ON PURIM AND AMALEK[132]

PREFACE

The Rav noted the paradoxical nature of Purim. On one hand, it is a joyous festival commemorating the miraculous salvation of the Jews from almost certain destruction. Thanksgiving, praise, and celebration mark this aspect of the day. On the other hand, the same occasion recalls a near-death experience that was interrupted only by divine intervention. Feelings of despair and plaintive pleas for compassion characterize this aspect.

Are these contrary dimensions unique to Purim or do they constitute an archetype for other

132. Based on Joseph B. Soloveitchik: "Towards the Metaphysical Significance of the Holiday of Purim," *Ten Da'at* 16 (2003), 69 ff. (henceforth: "Metaphysical"), adapted by Besdin *Reflections of the Rav*, 178 ff. as "Lessons in Jewish Survival," henceforth "Lessons."

circumstances? How should a Jew integrate these seemingly irreconcilable feelings into the marking of one and the same occasion?

The Rav explained this contradiction as an ordinary human condition. Fear and anxiety enable us to recognize that there is, indeed, evil in the world. Being cognizant of our predicament must instill in us humility, which can lead us out of jeopardy intact.

According to the Rav: "The Persian *galut* apparently was meant to provide lessons on how to survive as a people."[133] He listed four important lessons that must be learned from the story of Purim:

1. The human being, although created in a godly image, has the capacity to become evil, even satanic.
2. Amalek, the paradigm of evil, victimizes Jews more than others.
3. All Jews are subject to victimization, not only religious ones.
4. Amalek is eventually defeated and the Jewish people survive.

THE HALAKHIC PROPOSITION

In classical homiletic fashion, the Rav's first step was to establish a halakhic premise for a homily (*derashah*). In this case, that premise is that one is

---

133. "Lessons," 179.

obligated to read *Megillat Esther* twice: once at night and again during the day.

> R. Yehoshua ben Levi said: One is obliged to read the Megillah by night, and to read it again by day, as it says, "My God! I call by day and You do not answer, by night and I get no response from You" (Ps. 22:3). It was also said, by R. Helbo in the name of Ula Birah, that one is obliged to read the Megillah by night and to read it again by day, as it says, "Let honor sing Your praise and not be silent; the LORD, my God, I thank You eternally" (Ps. 30:13) (*Megillah* 4a).

Maimonides stipulated the identical conclusion, while omitting the prooftexts—as was his practice:

> It is a mitzvah to read [the Megillah] in its entirety and a mitzvah to read it by night and by day (*Hilkhot Megillah ve-Hanukkah* 1:3).

THE PHILOSOPHICAL SIGNIFICANCE OF THE HALAKHIC TEXT

The next step—equally typical of the Rav's classic homiletic style—was to demonstrate that the halakhic source he cited is not a "barren" legal formula but also a "pregnant" value statement. He accomplished this by distinguishing carefully between the two opinions cited in the Gemara ("We have before us one *halakhah* with two contradictory reasons") and attributing each to a separate motivation.

- R. Yehoshua ben Levi sees the *Megillah* as a prayer recited out of despair.
- R. Helbo sees it as a song of praise for deliverance from harm.

The Rav characterized the two approaches as follows:

R. Yehoshua ben Levi cites a verse from that famous chapter of Psalms, "My God, my God, why have You abandoned me" (22:3), a chapter which expresses the emotions of pain, deep frustration, and loneliness; a feeling of capitulation arises from these words…. They constitute words of prayer that give expression to an emotional state of deep depression, and a heartfelt plea to God to proffer assistance during this time of great crisis…. The reading of the Megillah is perceived as a prayer recited from despair, as a request for compassion and rescue.

R. Helbo cites a verse from "A psalm, a song of the dedication of the house, for

David," a chapter that expresses an attitude of
relief and satisfaction; the thanksgiving of a
man for whom a great miracle has occurred;
a chapter that contains expressions of wonder
and the most profound gratitude. [R. Helbo]
made his ruling because he apparently saw in
the reading of the Megillah a matter of psalm,
a song of praise for a miracle which occurred,
for which the Megillah must be read both by
night and by day.[134]

VICTORY AND JEOPARDY: A PARADOX

Purim, then, is a paradox (in the Rav's words: "a
dialectic"). He acknowledged its "two-faceted" nature
("a day of joy and thanksgiving, on the one hand, and
a day of prayer and soul-searching, on the other"),
again locating its origin in the Gemara:

> Rava said: One must become intoxicated on
> Purim until he cannot distinguish between
> "Haman is cursed" and "Mordechai is blessed"
> (*Megillah* 7b).

Yes. It is indeed a paradox, but—according to the
Rav—so is Judaism:

---

134. "Metaphysical," 69-70.

It appears paradoxical to mix together a song of victory with a prayer for compassion. But that is what we are: a paradoxical nation. Paradox is a part of our essence.[135]

This paradox is not exclusive to Purim. In fact, the Rav maintained that it is a feature of our daily prayers as well:

There is no clear or absolute distinction between a prayer of praise and one of request. We have no prayer that is exclusively one of praise and thanksgiving, without any trace of request or supplication. No matter how happy we are, how full of gratitude for the good portion we have been allocated, we cannot overlook the fact that we have no guarantee that the depression and the crisis in which we had been mired will not return and reappear. The joy and the thanksgiving, which often fill man's heart, cannot entirely expel his anxieties over the future.

Even the "Egyptian" Hallel contains chapters of joy and thanksgiving— "Halleluyah; Give praise you servants of the LORD," and "When Israel left Egypt"—on the one hand, and chapters of request and

135. "Metaphysical," 73.

supplication—"Not for us," "Please, O LORD, save us"—on the other. A kind of victory hymn—"Judah sanctified Him, Israel was His kingdom"—on one hand, and the prayer for supplication—"Please, O LORD, save us"—on the other.[136]

PURIM AS A *"DUGMA"* (PREFIGURATION[137]) OF JEWISH HISTORY

According to the Rav, we experience the paradox of victory and jeopardy daily.

> The fact of the Jews' exposure to danger is not just a tragic truth. It is more than that: Man's essential recognition that he is constantly exposed to danger nurtures several moral traits of a man who recognizes the fact that he lacks security.[138]

Furthermore, the Rav thought that *Megillat Esther* prefigures or foreshadows a recurring feature of Jewish history.

---

136. "Metaphysical," 72-73. See "The Rav on Prayer," above.
137. I have borrowed the term *dugma* from Rashi who utilized it throughout his commentary on *Shir ha-Shirim* to describe the relationship between the allegory of the song and the history it prefigures (or foreshadows).
138. "Metaphysical," 74.

Here I would like to note that the recognition that every creature is exposed to dangers finds its expression in *Megillat Esther* and it is very characteristic of the mode of Jewish life *in all the lands of their dispersion throughout all times.* In the Diaspora a Jew is always exposed to unanticipated dangers. The dread of sudden danger, however, is universal. Danger constantly stalks people, both as individuals and as political entities. I should also add here—without any connection to concrete events whatsoever—that this applies to the State of Israel, too, its ministers and military commanders, particularly as vicious enemies surround this state on all sides.[139]

What lesson are we supposed to learn from this constant paradox? As noted above, the Rav concluded that it is humility:

Man is naturally inclined towards pride and arrogance, towards aggression and standoffishness. The trait of humility is acquired only after bitter and difficult experience, when man reaches a clear conclusion that on account of his successes and attainments he is unremittingly exposed

139. "Metaphysical," 75.

to many and great dangers. Humility is the form of expression that such a process takes.[140]

Where do we see humility modeled in the story of Purim? In Mordekhai.

In the Megillah we read: "Each and every day, Mordekhai would stroll before the courtyard of the women's residence to find out how Esther was doing and what had become of her" (2:11). Had Mordekhai abandoned his humility to announce, publicly, that he was a close relative of Queen Esther, he would certainly have been treated with special respect by the masses, but then—the whole miracle of Purim would not have taken place. The miracle of Purim could take place only by virtue of Mordekhai's humility. Mordekhai's greatness expressed itself in the fact that he knew himself to be exposed to many dangers, and that in these situations, in particular, man must adhere ever closer to the trait of humility. A man's greatness is in direct proportion to his humility. The two are interdependent The miracle did not occur only on account of the virtue of Queen Esther; the modesty and humility of Mordekhai contributed no less.

140. "Metaphysical," 74.

His personality and feeling of responsibility influenced the reinforcement of his trait of humility.[141]

THE ABSURD AND THE ACCIDENTAL: THE TRUE LESSONS OF PURIM

The Rav asked:

- Do absurd and accidental things exist in nature or in history?
- Do we have the right to speak of fate or about luck as real factors in the record of a society?

As noted in our preface, the Rav then enumerated four "lessons" of Purim:

1. "Our faith in man must not blind us to the demonic within him."

From time to time human beings replace their personalities in which the image of God is implanted, with a personality in which Satanic deeds are noticeable. This discovery was, for the Jews of Persia, a traumatic moment, which they found very difficult to accept and to comprehend. This discovery is a no less difficult experience for all the Jewish

---

141. "Metaphysical," 74-75.

communities that encounter it throughout
the generations and in all eras. The Jew
believes that every creature possesses some
divine feature; that at all times and in all of
life's circumstances, something good reposes
in him and a divine spark still glows in his
personality.... Suddenly, the Jew discovers
that sometimes man can be transformed into
a real satanic personality, the symbol of evil
and corruption.[142]

2. "Every upheaval, every major movement and
event in history has dire possibilities for the Jews."

Amalek is the symbol of evil and the enemy
of mankind, in general, but first, foremost,
and especially, he attacks Jews. While illogical
and incomprehensible, it is an historical fact,
nevertheless, that Amalek hates Jews more
than any other nation, and is prepared to go
to greater lengths to cause them harm.... Jews
were not always aware of the dangers that lay
about them. They could not imagine that
manifestations of hatred or discrimination
towards them could take on catastrophic
proportions to the extent of the design of a
"final solution." ... In the Megillah we read

142. "Metaphysical," 78.

Haman's words: "Nothing is of any value to me whenever I see Mordekhai, the Jew, seated in the King's courtyard" (5:13). Haman couldn't stand the sight of Mordekhai the Jew, and this seemed sufficient reason for him to plan and implement destruction and annihilation....

My father used to tell me, in the name of his father, that those who give the fullest expression to the designs of Amalek are those wicked people who say: "Let us exterminate the Jewish people and the name of Israel will never again be heard" (Ps. 83:5). An unqualified anti-Semite is a descendant of Amalek, and is subject to the imperative of: "Surely eradicate the memory of Amalek." Amalek tries, relentlessly, to gather energy to commit genocide. The Nazi scourge and the Soviet oppressor are descended of Amalek.[143]

3. "A common destiny unites all Jews."

The same lesson... was learned by the Jews of Germany in the last generation, as well as by other Jewish communities in different lands and at different times. The lesson is that the hatred of Jews is not aimed only at the religious Jews alone, or specifically. It is aimed

143. "Metaphysical," 79.

at everyone who is known by the name, Jew. The hatred is directed towards Jews who are religious, secular, and even heretical; the Jew who is full of nationalistic Jewish feelings, and the Jew who tends towards integration and assimilation. Amalek hates *all* Jews.[144]

4. "God intercedes whenever total destruction faces the Jewish people."

Whenever the modern Satan-Amalek struggles with "the diffuse and scattered nation," there will surely arise a factor that will protect that nation, oppose Amalek with full force, and overcome him. I cannot name that factor, nor even describe its attributes, but I know that it acts in the name, and with the force, of divine providence.... In the case of Purim the agents—divine agents sent by God to fight Amalek-Haman—were Mordekhai, the Jew; the elderly, chastised survivor; and a young woman. The elderly man and the young woman were chosen by the Creator to undertake the rescue mission and they succeeded in forcing the enemy—with all his decisive influence in the kingdom of Persia and Medea—into submission.[145]

144. "Metaphysical," 80.
145. "Metaphysical," 81-82.

PURIM, PESAH, AND THE MESSIANIC AGE

> Rabbi Hillel said: The Jews have no Messiah,
> for they have already consumed him in the
> days of Hezekiah. Rav Yosef said: May God
> forgive Rabbi Hillel. When did Hezekiah live?
> During the first Temple. And yet Zachariah,
> who lived during the second Temple,
> prophesied: "Rejoice greatly, Daughter of
> Zion; Give cheer, Daughter of Jerusalem;
> Behold your king comes to you. He is
> righteous and a savior; poor and riding upon
> a donkey, upon the foal of an ass" (Zachariah
> 9:9) (BT *Sanhedrin* 98b).

The Rav asked: Is Rabbi Hillel denying the concept of
a human Messiah? The answer, he maintained, can be
ascertained from the following verses:

> God heard their cries and recalled His
> covenant with Abraham, Isaac and Jacob.
> God observed the Children of Israel and God
> knew. Moses was herding the sheep of his
> father-in-law, Jethro, the Midianite priest...
> (Exodus 2:24-3:1).

The proximity of these verses indicates that the
author of the drama of our redemption is God but

its principal actors are His human agents. God's recognition of the plight of the Jewish people launched the Exodus, but only after Moses agreed to serve as its captain.

> According to the Midrash, the negotiations between God and Moshe concerning his mission lasted for seven whole days, and there was no alternative because it was necessary for the proper agent to be appointed for the process of redemption to occur. Salvation always begins from a bitter and nerve-racking struggle between Amalek-Satan and the agent for the redemption. Without this mortal combat there is no opportunity for redemption. This is what our Master, Moshe, did at the time of the Exodus from Egypt, this is what Mordekhai and Esther did in Shushan, and this is what the King, Messiah, will do.[146]

The Rav's answer, then, to the question concerning Rabbi Hillel is:

> Rabbi Hillel did not, perish the thought, deny the matter of redemption; he only intended to say that God will reign, alone, and will bring salvation to Israel directly, without any need

---

146. "Metaphysical," 83.

for an agent of redemption. The difficulty in Rabbi Hillel's theory is unrecognizable to any of us. It would appear that the sequence of events during the redemption would be the work of the human agent. Redemption is a matter of agency; it consists of a principal and an agent.[147]

THE FINAL LESSON

Why was it necessary for the events of Purim to take place at all?

The Rav explained that the events of Purim, like those of our earlier enslavement in Egypt, were intended to educate us. Just as the enslavement in Egypt was designed to engender in us a concern for the unfortunate and unprotected, even non-Jews, the threat of extermination that hung over us in Persia was intended to promote a very particular brand of Jewish compassion (*rahmanut*). As he noted:

This is a sensitive Hebrew word, whose pronunciation, in Yiddish, gives it a special flavor. The expression: "*Yiddische rachmonus,*" says it all. Here is a characteristic expression for the special sensitivity and gentleness that mark the Jew and his outlook on the respect due to another.[148]

147. "Metaphysical," 82.
148. "Metaphysical," 84.

And he concluded:

> From their difficult and bitter history, Jews have learned sublime properties to which they became attached over the course of many generations and which became part of their nature. As it is with regard to the Exodus from Egypt—that we are not allowed to take our minds off it, and we must recall it daily— so it is, too, with the miracle of Purim. "And these days of Purim will never pass from among the Jews and their memory will never pass from their descendants" (Esther 8:28).[149]

---

149. "Metaphysical," 84.

EIZEHU GIBBOR?

HEROISM IN DAILY LIFE

PREFACE

Many of us imagine heroism, *gevurah*, to be a form of behavior limited to soldiers in battle or to people in circumstances of distress or persecution. We further imagine that heroism is displayed by only a few exceptional individuals (which is why we call them our "heroes") and most of us cannot imagine being called upon for acts of heroism given our ordinary, humdrum lives.

In "Catharsis," the essay on which this chapter is based,[150] the Rav made the point that heroism is a quality of which we are all inherently capable, and that truly heroic deeds can be performed even by ordinary people in their daily lives, provided that they are led according to *halakhah*.

---

150. *Tradition* 17:2 (Spring 1978), 38-54; see the Epilogue, below, on the significance of the title.

STRENGTH AND HEROISM

Question: Why do the daily morning blessings contain separate *berakhot* for *koʾah* and *gevurah,* when they seem to be practically identical? What is *gevurah* if not a particular manifestation of *koʾah?*

The Rav began by calling our attention to the distinction between *koʾah,* which he defined as physical strength and ability, and *gevurah,* which he deemed heroism. The former "denotes any aptitude which God has bestowed" upon either man or beast, while the latter is a uniquely human property. The former represents the force that inheres in all aspects of nature, while the latter is confined to "the human heroic gesture" that is undertaken in an "absurd" regard for common sense.

Curiously enough, even God is designated a *gibbor* in our prayers[151] because He, too, on occasion, has acted "contrary to human logic and practical judgment."[152]

Rabbi Yehoshua ben Levi said: Why were they called "The Men of the Great Assembly?"

---

151. Cf. the start of the second *berakhah* of the *ʿamidah*: אתה גבור לעולם ה'.
152. "Catharsis," 40.

Because they restored the crown of Torah as of yore. Moses proclaimed, "The great, valiant and awesome God" (Deut. 10:17). Then Jeremiah came and said, "With gentiles cavorting in His temple—where is His awesomeness?" (Jer. 32:18). So he deleted "awesome." Daniel came and said, "With gentiles ruling over His children, where is His valor?" (Dan. 9:4). So he deleted "valiant." Then came [the Men of the Great Assembly] and said, "Au contraire! His ultimate valor lies in His ability to overcome His inclinations and be long-suffering of evil" (*Yoma* 69b).

God has every right—we might even say the cosmic responsibility—to exercise His strength in the punishment of the wicked. Yet He abides by the same heroic code that is commended to man: "Who is a hero? One who conquers his [negative] inclinations" (*Avot* 4:1).

THE PATRIARCH JACOB, THE PARADIGM OF A HERO

Question: Why did Jacob, with victory within his grasp, relinquish his hold over his adversary and set him free?

The nighttime struggle that earned Jacob the name "Israel" ended in a paradoxical heroic gesture. On the verge of triumph, he relinquished his hold over a relentless adversary and allowed him to depart.

Jacob had every right—we might even say the moral responsibility both to himself and to his vulnerable family—to finish off his unprovoked attacker through the exercise of the same physical strength he had earlier displayed in removing the capstone from atop the well in Haran. His thoroughly unreasonable withdrawal from the encounter, with victory practically in hand, is the sign of the true hero.

In this context, the Rav briefly digressed to characterize the outstanding difference between the biblical and classical (Greek) notions of heroism. "The hero of classical man," he wrote, "was the grandiose figure with whom, in order to satisfy his endless vanity, classical man identified himself." "Biblical heroism," on the other hand, "is not ecstatic but rather contemplative, not loud but hushed, not dramatic or spectacular but mute."[153]

A DIGRESSION: HOMER AND THE BIBLE

Erich Auerbach, a classics scholar (and Jewish refugee from Nazi Germany), wrote an incisive critique of the differences between the depictions of heroism in biblical and classical literature. In a chapter entitled

---

153. "Catharsis," 42.

"Odysseus' Scar," he contrasted the exaggerated detail paid by Homer to his characters with the dearth of physical and psychological detail in the biblical story of the binding of Isaac (*'akeidat Yitzhak*). Note the example of such a contrast regarding the function of speeches:

> While speech, in the Homeric epics, serves "to manifest, to externalize thoughts," in the Bible it serves "to indicate thoughts which remain unexpressed"... Abraham's actions are explained not only by what is happening to him at the moment, nor yet by his character... but by his previous history; he remembers, he is constantly conscious of what God has promised him and what God has already accomplished for him—his soul is torn between desperate rebellion and hopeful expectation."[154]

Whether the Rav was directly influenced by Auerbach or made the observation on his own, we may prosper from his illustrious example in seeking to compare and contrast biblical characters with those we encounter in general literature.

---

154. *Mimesis: The Representation of Reality in Western Literature* (Princeton, 1974), 8-9.

HEROISM AS A "DIALECTIC"

The Rav described Jacob's heroism as "a dialectical performance," stating:

> The Torah wants man, who is bold and adventurous in his quest for opportunities, to act heroically, and at the final moment, when it appears to him that victory is within reach, to stop short, turn around, and retreat. At the most exalted moment of triumph and fulfillment man must forego the ecstasy of victory and take defeat at his own hands.... In a word, the Halakhah teaches man how to renounce, how to succeed, how to invite defeat, and how to resume the striving for victory.[155]

It should be borne in mind that the philosophical notion of the dialectic (characterized as: thesis-antithesis-synthesis), best known from the works of the German philosopher Hegel, also forms the foundation for the concept of Torah U'Madda (the presumptive ideology of Yeshiva University), which is also referred to as a "synthesis." The Rav, here, has taken the notion out of its original philosophical context and applied it, somewhat metaphorically, to the realm of action and behavior.

---

155. "Catharsis," 43-44.

HALAKHIC "HEROISM" IN DAILY LIFE

Question: While we know that *halakhah* regulates all aspects of religious and ritual law and behavior, does it also have a definition of what it takes to be a hero?

As noted above, the Rav maintained that everyone has the capacity to be a hero, and if *halakhah* is followed, heroic acts can be performed in each of the four principal dimensions of ordinary life. For example:

a) the *physical* realm, represented by marital relations
b) the *emotional* realm, represented by the laws of mourning
c) the *intellectual* realm, represented by science and scholarship
d) the *moral-religious* realm, represented by sin and repentance

Question (a): Can I be a hero if no one witnesses my heroism? Does heroism not, by definition, need public acclaim?

In the physical carnal realm, *halakhah* calls upon man and woman to be prepared, at even a moment's notice, to separate from one another, and to remain apart and withdrawn until it says that it is again permissible for them to reunite.

In a moving, almost poetic, passage, the Rav described the "movement of recoil":

> Bride and bridegroom are young, physically strong and passionately in love with each other. Both have patiently waited for this rendezvous to take place. Just one more step and their love would have been fulfilled, a vision realized. Suddenly the bride and groom make a movement of recoil. He gallantly, like a chivalrous knight, exhibits paradoxical heroism. He takes his own defeat. There is no glamor attached to his withdrawal. The latter is not a spectacular gesture, since there are no witnesses to admire and to laud him. The heroic act did not take place in the presence of jubilating crowds; no bards will sing of these two modest, humble young people. It happened in the sheltered privacy of their home, in the stillness of the night. The young man, like Jacob of old, makes an about-face; he retreats at the moment when fulfillment seems assured.[156]

---

156. "Catharsis," 45-46.

Question (b): Can someone be commanded to rejoice? Can someone who is busy rejoicing be commanded to stop and mourn? Can someone who is in mourning be commanded to set aside his sorrow and rejoice?

According to the Rav, not only does *halakhah* presume to instruct and direct our feelings—and not just our actions—but heroic deeds are as possible in the emotional realm as they are in the physical. The answers to the queries we posed above are yes, yes and yes.

In "rejoice in your festivals" (*ve-samahta be-haggekha*), the Torah commands us to rejoice. In "commemorate the destruction of the Temple" (*zekher le-hurban*), *halakhah* requires us to interrupt a joyous wedding ceremony in order to introduce a somber note of mourning. In the laws of mourning on Shabbat and Yom Tov, *halakhah* asks someone who is feeling the searing pain of the loss of the closest of relatives to separate himself from his feelings and return to the normal world.

The Rav illustrated this last point by means of the story of the High Priest Aaron who was instructed not to allow the deaths of his own two sons to interfere with his commitment to the consecration of the Tabernacle:

> Do not loosen the hair on your head, nor rend
> your garments, lest you die and He take out his
> wrath upon the whole congregation. Let your
> brethren, the whole house of Israel, bemoan
> the burning which the Lord kindled. Do not
> go out from the door of the Tabernacle, lest
> you die, for the anointing oil of the Lord is
> upon you. (Leviticus 10: 6-7)

In denying himself the "inalienable right" to which every parent is entitled, of mourning the death of a child, Aaron performed a heroic act. Heroism, in the emotional sphere, the Rav wrote, "consists in retreating or disengaging from oneself… in renouncing something that is a part of oneself… in active human interference with the emotive experience."[157]

> **Question (c):** In sections (a) and (b), we have seen that the Rav defined heroism as a form of withdrawal or self-abnegation. How does this apply to the intellectual realm, the world of knowledge and ideas?

Intellectual heroism, according to the Rav, requires two admissions on the part of the researcher or scientist. The first is that science can evaluate only

---

157. "Catharsis," 46-47.

the quantitative dimensions of the universe, but not its qualitative ones. Science can even offer theoretical constructs in explanation of natural phenomena, but it cannot account for the essence of being or existence. And second, no postulates of science, however laudable they may be in and of themselves, can replace Torah and *halakhah*. As he wrote:

> Any attempt on the part of scientific research, no matter how progressive, to replace the moral law engraved by the Divine hand on the two stone tablets of Sinai with man-made rules of behavior, is illegitimate. Adam tried to legislate the moral norm; he was driven from Paradise. In our day, modern man is engaged in a similar undertaking, which demonstrates pride and arrogance, and is doomed to failure.[158]

The intellectual hero, then, is neither the one who goes boldly towards the frontiers of the known world in search of the mysteries of the universe, nor the one who courageously propounds or defends unpopular theories. According to Torah and *halakhah*, he is the one with the humility to acknowledge "the unknowability of being," the true mystery of existence.

---

158. "Catharsis," 52.

If the scholar, simultaneously with the ecstasy of knowing, experiences also the agony of confusion, and together with the sweetness of triumph over Being, feels the pain and despair of defeat by Being, then his cognitive gesture is purged and redeemed. Then, and only then, does this gesture become heroic.[159]

Question (d): I always thought that the religious hero was the one who sacrifices his life to sanctify God's name. Is there any other kind of religious heroism?

The fourth and final realm that the Rav explored in this context is the moral-religious one. Just as heroism in the physical realm was characterized by withdrawal from a fellow being, emotional heroism by withdrawal from oneself, and intellectual heroism by withdrawal from the idea of ultimate knowability, so does religious heroism consist of the recognition that man, on account of his inherent imperfection, will often experience separation or withdrawal from his God. As he stated: "Sin is a reality, not just a potential threat."[160]

Indeed, the Rav pointed out that the Tanakh, "with ruthless honesty," records the failures of even

---

159. "Catharsis," 51.
160. "Catharsis," 54.

the greatest figures of antiquity,[161] because true religious heroism resides in "the aptitude of man to take a critical look at himself and to admit failure; in the courage to confess, to plead guilty; in the readiness to accept defeat."[162]

Every serious penitent, according to the Rav, is heroic. Acts of remorse, confession, and resolution can qualify each and every one as a religious hero.

EPILOGUE

The name the Rav gave to this exceptional essay, "Catharsis," may derive from either of two statements of the Sages that relate to this notion. The first is cited by the Rav himself:

> Rav said: The commandments were only given to purge [litzrof] men. For what difference does it make to the Holy One, blessed be He, if an animal is slaughtered from the neck or the nape? Say, rather, that commandments were only given to purge men (Vayikra' Rabbah, Shemini 13).

The second quotation is one quite familiar to those who study mishnayot, or who recite Pirkei Avot:

---

161. "Catharsis," 53.
162. "Catharsis," 54.

R. Hananiah ben Akashiah said: God wanted to purify [*lezakkot*] Israel, therefore did He give them Torah and *mitzvot*. As it is said: "It pleased the LORD, for the sake of His righteousness, to magnify Torah and make it honorable" (Mishnah *Avot* 6:11).

THE RAV ON *HAKAFOT*

ENCIRCLING THE
RITUAL AND THE ETHICAL[163]

PREFACE

If Sukkot is "our season of joy," then Simhat Torah is our "joy of joys." The completion of the annual cycle of Torah reading, the dancing, indoors and out, with all the Torah scrolls— these are some of the things many look forward to annually with great expectation.

The Rav taught us that there are several dimensions to the love we demonstrate towards the Torah and that the *hakafot*—literally, the encirclements—symbolize these relationships.

---

163. Based upon the Rav's essay: "Hakafot—Moving in Circles," in Abraham Besdin: *Man of Faith in the Modern World* (KTAV, 1989), pp. 150-160 (henceforth: "Hakafot").

WHAT DO WE ENCIRCLE?

There are three instances of *hakafot* in our tradition:

1. In the Temple, the altar was encircled by the people carrying the four species (*arba'ah minim*).
2. After the destruction of the Temple, and as a kind of commemoration, the people holding their four species would encircle the *hazan*, who would be holding a *Sefer Torah*.
3. Our present day custom to encircle the central platform (*bimah*) of the synagogue while holding the Torah scrolls.[164]

It is noteworthy that in the first two cases there is something or someone being encircled, whereas in the third case (as there is nothing on the *bimah*) there appears to be a circle around an empty space. Presumably, we would not waste effort encircling an empty center. Thus, the center must not really be empty; ergo, something is there, if not visibly, then symbolically. According to the Rav, "When nobody is there, Someone is there." Even when the center appears to be void, it retains the presence of God, and encircling it with Torah scrolls pays Him homage.

164. In Israel, *hakafot* are performed on the eighth day of Sukkot, on which Shemini Atzeret and Simhat Torah are combined. In the Diaspora, where the two holidays are celebrated on separate days, they are performed on Simhat Torah, although some Hasidic communities also perform them on Shemini Atzeret.

WITHOUT ETHICS, WE HAVE NOTHING

Can one fulfill a religious obligation by means of an unethical practice? For example: Can one fulfill the mitzvah of the four species with a stolen *lulav* even after the owner has become resigned to its loss and abandons his ownership of it?[165]

The answer is no. The Book of Psalms states: "I wash my hands in innocence, so that I may encircle Your altar, O Lord" (26:10). Rashi relates this verse specifically to the four species, saying: "The [mitzvah of the] four species may not be acquired through theft. A stolen *lulav* is invalid." What is the connection between innocence and encirclement? Before one approaches God, one must be sure that one's hands are "clean" in the spiritual sense.

The Rav pointed out that this concern for proper ethical conduct is a unique feature of Judaism. The ancient cults were unconcerned with ethics, only with results. Ancient societies may have imposed ethical codes on their citizens, but that was only for the purpose of preserving the social order. It was Abraham's ethical conviction that enabled him to

---

165. I have chosen this illustration because the text I cited links correct ethical practice specifically to *hakafot* that are performed on Sukkot. I emphasize *after* its abandonment by its owner because prior to that moment the *lulav* is still stolen property, making its use not merely a matter of ethics, but of law.

challenge God with: "Shall the whole world's judge not act justly?" (Gen. 18:25), and it is this same ethical conviction that enabled the prophet to state: "The Lord of Hosts is exalted through justice, and God, the Holy One, is sanctified through righteousness" (Isa. 5:16).

Does Judaism's concern for ethical treatment find expression only in matters of ritual law (like *lulav*)? Not at all; rather, this concern extends to all areas and walks of life.

ETHICS COUNT IN ACTION—NOT ONLY IN THEORY

Which *mitzvot* are more difficult to observe, the spiritual or the worldly?

In spite of the fact that some people tend to regard the "ritual" *mitzvot* as constricting and difficult to observe correctly, the Rav explained:

> Religious Jews, however, know that it is not tortuous to abstain from golf or shopping one day of the week, and that, on the contrary, the Sabbath is a rare jewel of spiritual and physical delight, an *oneg Shabbat*. Similarly, *kashrut* restrictions may, at times, be inconvenient, especially while traveling, but dieting for various reasons is common to many groups.[166]

166. "Hakafot," 152.

In fact, according to the Rav, the most difficult part of the *Shulhan Arukh* to observe is actually the "Laws of Jurisprudence" (*Hoshen Mishpat*). Can someone who acts unethically really be "religious"? In the opinion of our tradition, one who fails in his responsibilities to other people also fails in his responsibilities towards God. The Rav wrote:

> There are some who, though stringent in ritual observance, are less than meticulous in human relations. This, though inexcusable, may not be due to hypocrisy, but to the formidable standards of the *Hoshen Mishpat* with its demands that we discipline our greed in recognition of the rights and feelings of others. Even the mitzvah of *tzedakah*, to give charity, requires a readiness to lessen one's hard-earned equity for the sake of strangers, which is almost unnatural, and most find it difficult to observe properly.[167]

In our "post-modern" society, perhaps the gravest danger that lies in wait for us is the issue of the authority and validity of values. Ethics that are not founded on religious belief and practice can—and probably will—be relegated to the cultural trash heap by societies that place reason above revelation

---

167. "Hakafot," 153.

and that espouse a form of moral relativism, which, while it may be deemed politically correct, is often spiritually vacuous.

DO NOT DISMISS THE RITUAL

The significance of ethics notwithstanding, ritual is a vital aspect of religion. In the last two centuries, however, efforts were made to diminish the importance of ritual and to elevate the ethical to an even higher degree. The Rav continued with a restatement of the centrality that ritual occupies in Judaism—symbolized, in this instance, by the *hakafot* around the "empty" *bimah*. He inquired:

> There are modern Jews who, with genuine sensitivity and earnestness, are heard to ask: We are looking to experience God and you give us a Shulhan Arukh, telling us to *daven*, what not to eat, and how to conduct our marital lives. Why should we bog down in minutiae when we are searching for the infinite?[168]

God, he replied, is found in these so-called "minutiae." Far from being a pejorative term, "minutiae" are exactly what Judaism is about. Judaism is less concerned

---

168. "Hakafot," 154.

with transcendental experiences than with the here and now. Torah is this-worldly. As the Talmud states: "Torah was not revealed to the ministering angels" (*Berakhot* 25b)—and is far less preoccupied with otherworldliness. In the Rav's words:

> There is no royal road to God; it is a long winding road up steep hills. Instantaneous devoutness which envelops the soul only is not the Torah way.[169]

THE IMPORTANCE OF RECOGNIZING AUTHORITY

Does the authority of Torah derive from God, the Governor, or does it derive—to use American constitutional terminology—from "the consent of the governed"? What happens if the governed cease to consent?

Torah cannot be compared to man-made law. We have mentioned that there is an inclination in present-day society to dismiss ritual observance as irrelevant, or inferior, to spirituality. We also noted the tendency in our highly technological age to give greater consideration to science and reason than to revelation or religious law. Man today considers himself, subjectively, as supreme an authority in ethics and morality as he believes himself to be in matters

---

169. "Hakafot," 155.

of science and technology. Recognizing no authority greater than one's own, however, is antithetical to a genuinely religious personality.

The Rav, on the other hand, placed great emphasis on discipline and on authority. *Halakhah* (literally: a "path") denotes the acceptance of directions and instructions. Only when man looks to a source of authority outside of himself, only when he decreases his subjectivity and self-centeredness, only when he is open to the word of God without reservation, does he become a "Halakhic Man" (*Ish ha-Halakhah*).[170]

THE AUTHORITY (AND LIMITS) OF SCIENCE

What should be our response to science that has extended the frontiers of our knowledge in so many ways and of so many things? If it has been able to lead us, successfully, towards the understanding of the universe in unprecedented ways, why not defer to it in matters of ethics and morality as well?

Science has its legitimate place in the universe, but that place is distinctly subordinate to that of God. As noted in the previous chapter,[171] the Rav spoke of a kind of "intellectual heroism" that sharply curtails the prerogatives of science—one of the "deities" in our present day society's pantheon. First, he said, science

---

170. This is also the title of what many regard as the Rav's seminal work (published in 1983).
171. See "Who is a Hero?" above.

can evaluate only the quantitative dimensions of the universe but not its qualitative ones. In other words, science can offer theoretical constructs in explanation of natural phenomena but it cannot account for the essence of being or existence. Second, no postulates of science, however laudable they may be in and of themselves, can replace Torah and *mitzvot*. He wrote:

> Any attempt on the part of scientific research, no matter how progressive, to replace the moral law engraved by the Divine hand on the two stone tablets of Sinai with man-made rules of behavior, is illegitimate. Adam tried to legislate the moral norm; he was driven from Paradise. In our day, modern man is engaged in a similar undertaking, which demonstrates pride and arrogance, and is doomed to failure.[172]

THE LESSONS OF THE *HAKAFOT*

What should our attitude and approach be to those who do not share our appreciation of *halakhah* and its centrality?

According to the Rav, "All Jews count." During *hakafot*, he noted, all the marchers are always the same distance from the center, from God. "One may

---

172. "Catharsis," 52. See above, p. 171.

be Rabbi Akiba, another the Gaon of Vilna, and the next humble 'hewers of wood and drawers of water'—all have equal access to God."[173] The Rav also recalled the midrash that compared the four species to four different types of Jews (learned with good deeds, learned without good deeds, practitioners of good deeds without learning, and those with neither good deeds nor learning), and noted that only when they are all brought together can they be blessed. Similarly, he advocated outreach (kiruv) as a form of imitatio dei (resembling God) since He, too, is equally accessible to all the members of the circle.

Continuing with the imagery of a circle, just as the marchers are always equidistant from God at the center, it is also true that—like planetary travel—the periphery of a circle is always drawn towards the center. The altar symbolizes sacrifice, and the attraction of the marchers to the altar represents "the readiness to withdraw, to yield some aspects of one's freedom and indulgence in recognition of the Almighty, who is the source of all bounties."[174]

---

173. "Hakafot," 155-156.
174. "Hakafot," 157. The Rav also compared this to the Lurianic doctrine of tzimtzum.

CONCLUSION: *HAKAFOT*—WHERE PAST AND PRESENT MEET

A circle may be said to symbolize the unbroken continuity of Jewish history. Our forefathers lived not only in our past, but endure in our present as well—as illustrated by our symbolic invitation to them to be guests (*ushpizin*) in our *sukkot*. As the Rav concluded: "We greet them and bid them join our family in celebration. Our point of departure in the contemporary world is inextricably bound to our point of arrival from the past. We live in both simultaneously."[175]

---

175. "Hakafot," 159.

INDEXES

r-ʿ-h,	120 n.	28:11,	57
111		32:10-13,	24, 50 n.
sh-v-ʿ,	66	34, 56	
tehinah,	17, 25, 50	32:14,	56
tefillah,	see *p-l-l*	32:21,	83
		44:18,	27, 48

BIBLE

Genesis		**Exodus**	
1:12,	38	1:13-14,	62
2:5,	38, 39 n. 24, 41 n.	2:11ff,	73
26		2:11,	30
3:23,	85	2:23,	30, 66, 73
3:24,	85	2:24-3:1,	157
6:14,	82	2:24,	66, 87
12:18,	45	2:25,	86
15:18,	115	3:7,	87
18,	46	3:8,	114
18:1,	56	3:17,	114
17:17,	46	6:2,	66
18:22,	49	6:5,	66
18:23,	27, 49	6:7,	125
18:25,	47, 178	19:5,	109
19:1,	56	19:9,	84
19:27,	57	19:20,	19
20:7,	45, 47	21:22,	17
22:5,	143	21:24,	124
24:63,	57	24:7-8,	126
24:67,	111	25:17ff,	83

NAMES

Ahrend, Moshe,   100
Auerbach, Erich,   164-165
Auerbach, Shlomo Zalman, 42
Berman, Saul,   26 n. 14, 28
Bloom, Benjamin,   88 n. 73, 94
Chelst, Kenneth,   64
Dorson, Richard,   65
Dunbar, Laurence,   64 n. 55s
Fox, Everett,   39
Franklin, Benjamin,   63
Gardner, Howard,   94
Geiger, Yitzhak,   11
Greenberg, Moshe,   23, 56
Guttman, Julius,   9
Hegel, G.W.F.,   166
Heschel, Abraham Joshua, 12, 93, 95, 97-98, 102
Kane, Jeffrey,   94, 103
Kaplan, Aryeh,   95
Leibowitz, Nehama,   64 n. 54, 15 n. 106
Leibowitz, Yeshayahu,   12, 95-97
Lichtenstein, Aharon,   104
Muffs, Yohanan,   47
Nasser, Gamel Abdel,   124
Peli, Pinchas,   10, 119 n. 110
Pushkin, Alexander,   10
Shapira, Kalonymus Kalman, 92

Made in the USA
Monee, IL
12 November 2020

47328158R00121